Course Design and Construction for Horse Trials

Course Design and Construction for Horse Trials

ALL PHASES · ALL LEVELS

Compiled and Edited by
Mary Gordon Watson

THE KENILWORTH PRESS

First published in Great Britain by
The Kenilworth Press Ltd
Addington
Buckingham MK18 2JR

© The Kenilworth Press Ltd 1987
Reprinted 1991 and 1993

Designed by Alan Hamp
Editorial Assistant: Suzannah Staley

Typeset by MS Filmsetting Limited, Frome, Somerset
Printed and bound in Great Britain by
Butler & Tanner Ltd, Frome and London

British Library Cataloguing in Publication Data

Course design and construction for horse trials:
    all phases, all levels.
    1. Courses (Horse sports)—Design and construction
    I. Gordon-Watson, Mary
    798.2'4   SF294.35

    ISBN 0-901366-13-7

Contents

Introduction 7

The Principles of Course Design *by Patrick Lynch* **13**

Designing the Course *by Hugh Thomas* **17**
The Site 17
  a) The Going 17
  b) Natural Features 20
  c) Using the Terrain Provided 21
  d) Layout of the Course 23
  e) Siting the Fences 26

Designing the Obstacles *by Hugh Thomas* **30**
Schooling Fences 44
Portable Obstacles 46

Constructing the Obstacles *by Philip Herbert* **47**
General Points 47
Labour 50
Equipment 51
  a) Vehicles 51
  b) Machinery 52
  c) Tools 56
Timber 65
Dimensions 68
Types of Obstacle 70
  a) Posts and Rails 70
  b) Variations of Posts and Rails 81
  c) Fences with Post and Rail Framework 90
  d) Posts and Rails for Alternatives and Combinations 94
  e) Other Types of Fence 96
  f) Walls 103
  g) Brush Fences 104
  h) Birch Fences 108
  i) Steeplechase Fences 118
  j) Ditches and Banks 120
  k) Water Obstacles 139

**PART I
The
Cross-Country**

Options, Alternatives and Combinations
by Neil Ayer **151**

Recommended Distances **168**

Competition Organisation and Control
by Hugh Thomas **171**
    a) Checking the Cross-Country Course and Fences   171
    b) Communications   171
    c) The Start and Finish Area   171
    d) Flags and Other Markers   174
    e) Roping   177
    f) Spectators   177
    g) Penalty Zones   178
    h) On-Course Repairs and Adjustments   178
Communications and Control System   179

Three-Day Events *by Hugh Thomas* **182**
Roads and Tracks   182
Cross-Country Box   183
Steeplechase   186

The Rider's View of the Cross-Country Course
by Mary Gordon Watson **189**

PART 2
Dressage

The Dressage Arena *by Mary Gordon Watson* **197**
The Site   197
Layout   198

PART 3
Show Jumping

Show Jumping *by Richard Jeffery* **207**
Course Designer's Brief   207
The Arena   207
Equipment and Materials   208
Officials   209
Planning and Designing the Course   210
Building the Course   222

Making Your Own Show Jumps   227

Acknowledgements   233

Index   235

Introduction

The purpose of this book is to provide expert advice of the highest standard for course designers, course builders and — to some extent — organisers of Horse Trials at all levels, from local club competitions to International Three-Day Events. In particular it offers a practical, easy-to-follow guide to the design and construction of cross-country fences.

As Horse Trials have developed into a more sophisticated sport, in which only riders with a highly professional approach can excel at the top levels, courses have become more complicated and technically demanding. It is tempting, therefore, for course designers to become more and more ambitious, devising more and more complex obstacles. Mindful of such temptations, the contributors to this book are unanimous in their aim: to design and build courses which are sound, safe and acceptable to all competitors in all conditions.

Most of the fences which we recommend may be expensive to build and many people may not be able to afford treated timber, or the best machinery or tools, or major earthworks, but economy will not pay and a solid, well-built obstacle will be a good investment. It will stand up to constant use in all weathers, year after year, as well as encouraging safe, confident jumping.

The future of the sport is largely dependent on the successful design and construction of the fences. In this book we try to safeguard that future by giving detailed advice on the many pitfalls to avoid — thus saving time, labour, expense and possible injury.

All the contributors are Horse Trial enthusiasts who

devote a major part of their lives to this sport.

Patrick Lynch has worked closely with Jack Le Goff, the eminently successful trainer of the United States Equestrian Team for so many years.

Hugh Thomas, who rode for Great Britain in the Montreal Olympics of 1976, is designer of the Olympic Three-Day Event in Korea 1988. His wide experience covers all aspects of eventing, from Pony Club to International level.

Philip Herbert has also emerged at the top of his profession, having served a thorough apprenticeship, much of it under Bill Thomson who has probably been responsible for more good cross-country obstacles than anyone else in the world. Philip is a craftsman who takes enormous pride in his fence construction, whatever the standard of competition.

The services of Neil Ayer are sought all over the United States, and he designed the course for the World Championships in Australia in 1986, as well as the Los Angeles Olympic Games. He is also the organiser of the popular Ledyard Horse Trials at his home in Massachusetts.

Richard Jeffery designs show jumping courses throughout the United States, in Great Britain, and elsewhere. He is renowned for his careful planning and conscientious attention to detail.

Mary Gordon Watson

Part 1
THE CROSS-COUNTRY

The Principles of Course Design

Whether designing and building a full-scale cross-country course for a competition, or a few useful schooling fences, it is essential to know and understand the particular requirements before you start. Every course designer will have developed his own philosophy on the principles of building a good course. He should never lose sight of his objectives, however difficult this might prove to be in practice. In a competitive cross-country event the aim of the course will vary in emphasis according to the standard of the horses and riders taking part. It may be to teach, to test, or to entertain; preferably a blend of all three. At the lower levels, the emphasis should be on teaching, and at advanced levels it should be much more on testing. Whatever the level, the designer should prepare a course that is safe, practical and enjoyable for horses, riders and spectators.

Probably the most important quality needed by a course designer is horse sense, which can only be acquired after many years of knowing and working with horses. This must be combined with an inordinate amount of common sense — which is something that you are born with. Together, these two attributes should ensure that a designer does not allow his ego to over-ride his basic knowledge and sound judgment. He is not in competition with riders or other course designers, but in partnership with them — providing a means by which horses can be systematically trained and brought to their full potential. If he allows his ego to take control, the desire to out-smart may rebound on him, and the innocent victim will be the horse; the demand for his services as a designer may then cease! The most successful course designer is invariably one who has a sound working knowledge of horses. He should watch and study them jumping across country and in the show ring as often as possible, and try to get the 'feel' of how a horse uses his body, legs and mind in different situations. As well as observing how they perform physically, he should watch and learn from occasions when a horse appears to receive a distorted image of what is in front of him; see how he reacts, and be influenced accordingly when designing fences. The science of course designing cannot be exact, so the better your feel for horses and the way they move over the ground, the better are your chances of providing a good course.

If one hundred designers were to plan a course over any one stretch of land, they would produce one hundred different tests. The best would invariably be those designed by the inspired horseman, but as inspiration is something that cannot be taught, the rest of us have to learn from observation, trial and (only occasionally, one hopes) error. Whether you are a beginner or a more experienced designer, the following are some of the basic principles that should be followed.

Before you start to design a course, make sure that the site is suitable for the particular level and type of competition to be run. The length and difficulty of the course may have to comply with certain rules, especially in official Horse Trials where the standard demanded by a particular class or grade must always be maintained. There must be suitable locations for parking, for competitors, and for the public, as well as sites for dressage and show jumping.

To make the most of the land available, you must explore the entire area, getting to know its features and acquiring a feel for it. Talk to the people who ride regularly in the area and those who own and look after it. Find out what the condition of the land and the weather are likely to be at the time of the competition. Although climatic conditions are often variable and unpredictable, it is essential to know what may reasonably be expected. Whether it is English spring rain, American summer heat, or Australian dry season, it will have a major effect on the way that the course will ride. If the site is liable to extremes of wet or dry weather, it is usually better to build a course elsewhere, rather than spending a lot of time, energy and expense on an elaborate course and then being forced to cancel the competition. Alternatively, it could be held at a more suitable time of year.

Next, the route of the course must be planned, using as many of the natural advantages as possible; it is hills and valleys, ditches, streams and banks that make the cross-country much more than just a long show jumping course.

Once you have laid out a good track which avoids natural hazards you must now ensure that you do not produce your own man-made traps. How to decide which conceptual design is safe and which is not is difficult to define, as every situation differs. The actual construction of a safe course is basically a matter of skilful technique — using big, solid materials, and paying careful attention to every detail.

Whatever the problems, the designer's main consideration must be to safeguard the horse, who didn't ask to compete. If the rider carries out his function satisfactorily — which is above all to stay on the horse — you will be safeguarding him, too. It may be stating the obvious, but never design a fence that invites a fall; enough grief is already brought about by headstrong or poorly ridden horses.

Instead, you must accurately assess the degree of boldness, training and horsemanship required for the level of competition for which you are designing the course.

The next aim is to produce a cross-country test that rewards the best trained, best ridden horse, and to do it without overstepping the bounds of safety for the lesser horses and riders. This is not easy to achieve, particularly at the lowest levels, where the designer has to reduce the challenge to match the limited experience and skills of the competitors. He must provide a variety of obstacles that will 'teach' without asking for more than natural boldness and basic riding skills. At the higher levels, where the horse's and rider's experience is developing, a greater degree of boldness can be expected, as can greater skill in negotiating combinations, related fences, and more challenging terrain. At this level you are asking questions which will determine how well a horse has been trained and how competently he is ridden. You will be testing not only his boldness, but how controllable a horse is by asking him to turn in either direction, to shorten and lengthen his stride, and to hold a straight line.

In Horse Trials the degree of difficulty of the cross-country test is related to that of the dressage and show jumping. As cross-country and show jumping courses are becoming more and more technical, it is therefore essential for the course designer to study and understand the dressage tests to be used in the different divisions of an Event, so that he can maintain a suitable balance between the phases.

When planning a course you must remember that the result of the competition will be decided not only by penalties incurred through falls or refusals, but also from time lost through failure to take the shortest, smoothest line. For this reason, the course must be measured as accurately as possible, particularly at the higher levels, where time related to distance travelled has a greater bearing on the outcome of the Event. The distance should be calculated by walking the shortest route that a horse might take. There is no point in building a more demanding short route if no time penalties are incurred by taking the much longer and easier route.

It must also be remembered that other types of penalty may be paid by a horse, although they do not show on the score sheet. His legs may suffer if he is ridden too fast or without balance over rough terrain, up or down hills, and at the obstacles. Too often damage is inflicted on a horse's mouth when his rider tries to bring him back or to make a sharp turn. These penalties may be due to bad riding but they should never be due to bad course building. If the designer understands the logical progression from lower to international level, the intelligent rider will be able to upgrade a young horse gradually to an advanced standard while preserving a soft mouth and developing the skill to negotiate the more technical obstacles without hauling on his teeth. Of course, systematic progress through the different levels is not just designed to protect horses' mouths; it will also build and maintain confidence.

Steady progression is also important in the design of the course itself. The horse should be allowed to move into a rhythm on the cross-country before reaching a major obstacle, and the other challenging fences should be spread out evenly over the course — ending with one or two designed to inspire confidence, so that horse and rider will start their next cross-country competition in the right frame of mind. The problems posed should be of equal significance throughout the course. No one obstacle should be designed to have a particular influence or impact. This balance will not only be of benefit to the competitors but also to the spectators and those controlling them. If riders dislike an obstacle when walking the course because it appears particularly difficult or trappy they may not ride it with confidence, and this will be transmitted to the horse; riders could also lose concentration at the easier fences before or after it. When one fence causes several falls or refusals this can have a bad effect on subsequent competitors. Inevitably, spectators will flock around such a 'black spot'.

A horse's speed, stamina and ability to jump a big fence are not the course designer's main concern. The emphasis should be on the rider's skill — or lack of it — in training and riding his horse, and not on the horse's inborn ability. The cross-country should not be designed to show how fast a horse can go but to test the control and use of speed combined with the horse's other capabilities. Stamina and the ability to jump big fences should only be put to the test in a Three-Day Event.

Having satisfied yourself that you will be able to provide a safe course suitable for the level of competition, which will improve the skills of horse and rider while at the same time testing them, you must then turn your attention to the spectators. The course designer will be well aware that these are often his greatest critics. An intelligent designer should listen to any criticisms and suggestions with an open mind, whether it comes from an expert or a novice. He should always be willing to accept responsibility for a mistake and make every effort not to repeat it.

The most interesting obstacles should be as accessible to the public as possible, but their crowd-pulling merits should be secondary to their competitive function. With a little ingenuity it is possible to achieve both.

Ultimately it is on the skill of the course designer and builder that the success or failure of all the phases in a competition depend, whether it is a Pony Club Horse Trial or an International Three-Day Event. The good name and continuing popularity of the sport itself is our responsibility; memories of a bad course or a bad fence last a lot longer than those of courses and fences which ride fairly and well.

Designing
the Course

The choice of suitable terrain on which to site a cross-country course will be governed by the standard and length required. An ideal site for Novice Horse Trials or Pony Club Hunter Trials, for instance, could well be useless for a major International Three-Day Event, and vice-versa. When inspecting the site, remember that though *you* may be walking, the horses will be galloping, so avoid rocky or hazardous ground which will interfere with the flowing continuity of the course. Open, slightly undulating terrain which incorporates some interesting natural features is recommended.

THE SITE

(a) The Going

The going is the most important factor of all when choosing the site for a cross-country course. Over the last two decades the importance of this has become generally accepted, and standards have improved dramatically.

Even at the lowest levels, competitors now look for the best possible conditions, and are learning to avoid the unnecessary risk of running their horses on unsuitable ground — whether it be too deep, too hard or too rough. Given good ground conditions, horses will last much longer and enjoy cross-country better, thus providing more fun for their riders.

Well-drained ground is essential, particularly in areas where prolonged or sudden heavy rain is a possibility.

PERMANENT GRASSLAND provides the most suitable going. Old pasture, as found in Britain's parklands and which may never have been ploughed, is best of all. Its springy turf withstands wear and tear, generally drains well, and does not bake too hard in summer.

The type of soil underlying the grass is of critical importance, and even more so in places where there is no thick grass covering, such as on tracks or in wooded areas.

CLAY LAND is generally unsuitable for a cross-country course. In dry weather it will bake and crack; after rain it can become very sticky and holding. Although the comparative heaviness or lightness of clay varies according to area or country, this type of ground seldom provides consistent or satisfactory going, and should therefore be avoided.

SAND-BASED SOIL can provide the ideal cross-country footing, especially when it has a good covering of grass on it, as it will withstand almost any variation in weather conditions. It is rarely too hard, and it drains extremely well. A good example of this is the excellent site at Luhmühlen in West Germany, venue of many international championships, where the horses always seem to run particularly well.

It should be noted, however, that some types of sandy ground can be deceptively unyielding, or 'dead' — causing strain and lameness to horses — and are therefore less suitable. Examples of this may be found where the sand has no grass cover, or when it is packed hard, or it is too deep, or inconsistent.

CHALKLAND, LIMESTONE AND OTHER STONE-BASED SOILS are variable, but they almost certainly provide more suitable terrain than clay. During dry weather these types of ground become very hard, while after a light shower the grass on top can become slippery. Any chalk or stone-based soil tends to be thin and needs a thick covering of grass to provide enough grip for the horses' hooves and to protect their feet from flints or stones that could cut or bruise them. Land which has sharp stones lying above the surface should not be used. Generally, however, in all but the driest conditions, chalkland can be regarded as suitable for a cross-country course.

VOLCANIC AND ALLUVIAL SOILS are extremely good ground for horses as long as the land is well-drained. Volcanic soil is generally found on the slopes of hills and should therefore drain easily, but alluvial soils are likely to be found in valleys and river basins where drainage can be a problem. To determine whether such an area would be suitable, the site should be inspected during the *worst* possible conditions.

LOAM — a rich soil ideal for gardening — provides excellent ground for cross-country. It is a compound of sand, clay, humus and silt, found in varying proportions throughout the world, and it usually has a thick grass covering.

☐ Ideal going is that which will be *reliable* in any weather conditions, whereas bad ground is seldom of use for cross-country competition or practice. However, most land is more suitable for use at certain times of the year, and this is an important factor to consider when fixing the date of the Event. Obviously, this must comply with the landowner's wishes, but he, too, will be aware of the risk involved in using his land during a period when its condition is liable to be unpredictable. All too often, a competition which has an excellent cross-country course built on good ground is ruined by 'unexpected' heavy rain or an 'unusual' dry spell.

☐When selecting a site for a course or an Event, or if you are planning a course on a site already chosen, do not believe any assurance that 'it never rains here in August'. It is essential for you to take the trouble to view the site under the most adverse conditions possible and to make certain that the ground is suitable, by discussing it with reliable people who have actually ridden horses over it in extremes of dry weather and wet.

Perfect conditions are rare. From the outset you should be prepared for the worst, and consider what action to take should the going become unsuitable because of bad weather.

Ground that bakes hard is generally much easier to deal with than very soft, holding, going where even putting down substantial quantities of stonedust, or similar material, is unlikely to be satisfactory except perhaps to reduce the slipperiness. Look into the practicalities of harrowing, rolling, rotivating, or watering the ground. The most difficult to deal with is stony, flinty ground, where, for example, rotivating the soil to provide a galloping track will expose the stones which will then have to be removed by hand or covered with an artificial material or a layer of sand.

In extreme cases, such as when the going might become too deep, or for major competitions, you may even consider putting in new drainage or artificial take-offs/landings and galloping tracks. Such remedies are expensive and must be used only as a last resort.

☐Artificial take-offs and landings can be made successfully by using a separating material such as terram (a type of fibre matting) covered with sand, soil, stone or similar material. Although this somewhat unnatural and costly procedure provides a good long-term solution, always remember that on any cross-country course the track between the fences covers a far greater distance than the small area which surrounds the obstacles, and there is no point in having good take-offs and landings without providing adequate galloping conditions in between.

☐A course designer must have full knowledge of the non-competitive uses of the land on which his course is to be planned. Is it used for grazing, and if so for what animals? Does the farmer, or landowner, take hay off it? Are crops grown, and if so what are they? Is the use of any particular field likely to be repeated permanently or will it rotate from year to year or every two to three years? All such matters must be discussed with the landowner before any course design work is undertaken. What you see in front of you on a first visit may have changed significantly by the time of the competition, and certainly may not resemble the conditions that will prevail on the same site three to five years later.

☐Grassland used for grazing obviously provides the most suitable going, but avoid ground poached by livestock, particularly young cattle. Permanent pasture grazed by sheep is usually ideal, as long as they are moved off it soon enough ahead of the competition itself so that the grass will not be cropped too short; otherwise it is liable to become slippery or hard.

19

In those parts of the world where they abound, beware of rabbits! Holes made by them or by other animals are a menace, and you should always assume that another rabbit will soon excavate a new hole very close to the old one which you have just filled in.

Occasionally it may be necessary to cross a piece of arable farmland. Light plough or a short stubble field are perfectly acceptable, but heavy plough or a field of coarse, strong stubble would be damaging to a horse's legs. Few landowners would allow horses to cross a sown field, but given adequate warning and incentive might be persuaded to leave a headland around the edge of a field.

☐ Woodland provides useful and enjoyable variety on a cross country course, but can be very difficult for the course builder. The going is likely to be much more treacherous than one might imagine, and, in particular, leaf mould gives deceptive footing. Woodland does not normally drain well, and can become very deep and surprisingly holding for horses. Remember that a horse weighs some half a ton, so calculate the force with which his foot will land in the deep ground, at some 20–30 mph (32–48 kph) and from a height of four to six feet (1.2 to 1.8 m). The depth caused by this force cannot be compared with sticking the heel of your boot in the ground! Well grassed woodland-rides are usable provided the underlying soil is suitably sound, but narrow tracks should obviously be avoided if possible. Try to ensure that there is a variety of routes that the horses may take through a wooded area, so that no one particular patch will get too poached. At certain times of day and in bad weather the visibility in dense woodland must also be considered.

☐ It is most important that the going throughout a cross-country course should be as consistent as possible. Changes in the type of going, whether it be from hard to soft, from long grass to short, from woodland paths to hard tracks, can cause serious damage to a horse's legs. Sometimes, although no one particular bad area may be responsible, the overall effect of too many variations in the going can be harmful.

Where a river or stream is a feature of the course, the water level could be crucial. If a river should flood, this might affect several of the other obstacles sited near by.

Finally, when selecting the terrain and exact site for your course, always remember that the crucial factor could be the weather, and plan the date of your competition with this foremost in your mind.

(b) Natural Features

In looking for a really good site for a cross-country course, its natural features are almost as important as the going, already discussed. Undulating land is ideal, while steep hills or totally flat ground should be avoided. Too many hills restrict the course designer, because he will have to plan a route and fences which avoid undue stress on the horses. Flat ground, on the other hand, imposes demands on his imagination that may be difficult to meet.

Flat ground obviously will be needed for dressage, show jumping and other activities, but gentle slopes and rolling countryside are what the cross-country course designer will look for. Several long uphill pulls will be more taxing on horses than short, sharp slopes. The latter will also be much easier from the point of view of fence design, as they can be used for impressive drop fences, steps and many different and imaginative obstacles.

After the all-important going, the main consideration in looking at a piece of countryside will be whether obstacles can be fitted into it naturally. Suitable terrain would include some undulations, any natural hedges, walls, banks, or field boundaries typical of the area, a suitable pond or lake, and rivers and natural ditches which might run across the site. Lanes or tracks, and even buildings, can be incorporated into obstacles, while a pit, dell or quarry can be a particular asset, as can a depression in the ground — suitable for an obstacle such as a sunken road or a coffin.

A good course will almost design itself, so that each fence will fit in naturally and easily, and the course builder will only need to create one or two obstacles from his imagination.

Where natural features are plentiful you should avoid the temptation of using *all* the interesting ones, as this would be likely to make the overall course far too taxing. All course designers should be aware of this temptation when making their initial plans. When selecting suitable features it is also important to think of the spectators. At a major Event, the position of television cameras may also need careful consideration. Both the human eye and the electronic eye require good vantage points, and fences grouped around small hillocks or in the bowl of a valley may well provide a superb setting. A thick woodland area, however, though offering some good sites for obstacles, is often inaccessible to spectators, as well as to official and emergency vehicles.

(c) Using the Terrain Provided

A sensible course designer might rule out a particular site for reasons such as lack of space, unsuitable going, or difficult access. However, even though conditions may generally be more favourable than this, the designer must accept that his site is not perfect and must therefore make the very best use of it.

He will first of all have to consider the going, and will have to decide (a) where to site his obstacles and (b) the general layout of the competition. If there is the slightest doubt about the going in a particular place, do not put an obstacle there. On difficult sites it is sometimes necessary to find all the suitable pieces of ground, to build obstacles on them, and then to connect them up as best one can. In such circumstances the more testing obstacles should be sited on the soundest and preferably the flattest ground.

☐ Hills on a site where the going is also difficult will be much more demanding and will therefore have a greater influence on the competition, as well as making considerable demands on the course designer, who will want to avoid having too many drop fences or uphill obstacles.

A course built on very hilly terrain with a high proportion of drop fences or fences going across the side of a slope puts a strain on the horses' legs. Having to go uphill too often is also very tiring. To minimise the amount of stress caused to the horses it is often possible to follow the contours of the hills rather than to go straight up or down them. However, in skirting around a hill, a steep lateral slope may still subject the horses' legs to considerable strain. On any hilly site the designer will not be able to avoid an uphill climb or two, but these should not be right at the beginning or — even more important — at the end of the course. Given the choice, it is preferable to include hilly terrain in the early part of the course, and to allow the horses to run on fairly flat ground when they are getting tired. Do not assume that hills are any less stressful at Novice, Pony Club, or Riding Club levels simply because the course is fairly short. With relatively inexperienced or unfit horses and riders, a hilly course can have more influence than at more advanced levels.

☐ Another important factor to bear in mind when designing fences on a difficult site is that their width and the choice of take-off areas will greatly influence the competition. If several hundred horses have to jump a fence from the same take-off on going that is deteriorating through the day the course designer has not provided a test which is fair to *everyone*. It is all too easy to forget this factor when producing an imaginative design. Too often a large amount of timber is used for building an obstacle which offers several optional routes but only one that is actually viable, and by 2 o'clock in the afternoon this becomes a bog!

☐ The area required for a course varies considerably, according to the type of terrain. In principle, a 50 to 70-acre (20 to 28-hectare) farm will often provide enough land for a 1–1½ mile cross-country, as long as most of the land is usable for the course. For example, the inclusion of some boundary fences or wet areas may entail considerable expenditure. On the other hand, if you have, say, 500 acres (200 hectares) at your disposal there should be a greater opportunity to make the course more natural, so that it includes whatever obstacles happen to be on the particular route you have chosen. For spectators it is worth remembering that a course which covers one big circle will probably include very few fences that can be seen from one vantage point. A 'clover leaf' pattern provides a much more satisfactory course for those watching. This is a series of loops which go out from the start and back almost to the centre again, two or perhaps three times.

The designer should not be afraid of laying his route in such a way that at times it appears nearly to cross itself, or zig-zags. As long as careful thought is given to the fences — making the most of natural features — it is amazing how small an area can be used for a cross-country course.

When a course is very twisty, the designer must consider how he can make it 'flow'. The positioning of turns is crucial. Although gentle curves are best because they ride more easily, sharp turns are made easier when they are sited just after, or even just before, an obstacle rather than breaking up the gallop between obstacles.

(d) Layout of the Course

Before you start to plan the layout of your course, find an up-to-date, detailed map of the site, and, if possible, a good aerial photograph. Study the terrain, noting the contours of the hills, wooded areas, fence lines, roads or tracks, and any significant features such as streams and ditches. In particular, look for the best access points to the site for horses, spectators and officials. These, and the routes available for emergency services, are of vital importance, and in many cases it will be the position of a surrounding road, or a track within the site, which will have the greatest influence on the eventual layout.

□ When setting up a new Event site, plan the ideal route for the cross-country first, and then modify it, as necessary, to fit in with the requirements of the dressage and show jumping as well as the parking areas and other amenities. This is preferable to laying out a basic site and then seeing if the cross-country will fit around it.

When you inspect a bare site in mid-winter it may be difficult to imagine how it will look on the day of the competition, with all the tents, cars, horses and people there. Now is the time to assess whether the area available is really large enough for your purpose.

□ Visualising the ideal route for your cross-country course, you should use the large-scale map to mark out, as accurately as possible, the space required for the show jumping ring, dressage arenas, practice areas, horsebox and car parking, catering tents, and tradestands.

□ Good, flat ground is essential for dressage. At most Three-Day Events the same area will be used for the show jumping phase.

□ At One-Day Events it is essential to have dressage arenas in a quiet place, well away from galloping or jumping horses.

□ Do not underestimate the amount of space needed for the collecting or warm-up areas for dressage and show jumping. All Events must provide an area where at least two practice fences can be jumped in safety. Ideally, a separate paddock should be used for this.

□ A large One- or Three-Day Event site must also provide suitable areas for tradestands, or even a large tented village for traders.

□ Next, consider the aesthetic appearance of the site. For example, if the course is on land around a large house, it is important that interesting fences should be built in the area facing the house. If there are any natural grandstands from which spectators can view a variety of obstacles, these should be used to best advantage.

□ Once you have walked a site thoroughly and are familiar with all its features, the best method of laying out the site is to use your large-scale map, and cut-outs — representing the various arenas and tents,

The Leaf Pit at Burghley, built into a natural woodland 'bowl'. It has a steep drop but a smooth take-off and landing.

for instance — which can be moved around the map. To help you achieve the right distance and route, a piece of string cut to the correct length according to the scale of the map will be a great help; it is particularly useful in the early planning stages, as it can be easily adjusted and can be fixed with drawing pins to follow any route which you are considering. The string will not, of course, give a precise distance; this can only be measured accurately with a wheel or tape on the actual site. On a flat site, the course could cover the maximum distance allowed, whereas if the site is hilly and trappy, the course will have to be shorter.

☐ Having considered all the relevant factors, you can now decide on the actual route that the course will take. When more than one competition is being run, the course lengths will vary accordingly, but the Start and Finish line of the cross-country can be the same for all classes.

☐ In planning the route for courses of any standard, always ensure that the Start and Finish are over terrain which is not too testing. On the early part of the course, encourage competitors to establish a rhythm on reasonably flat ground, and avoid an uphill pull or steep descent until at least two obstacles have been jumped and the horses have got into their stride. The middle section of the course, when horses are settled but not too tired, should be the most demanding. Again, avoid steep hills, either up or down, over the last quarter to half mile.

□A complete knowledge of the rules for the particular competition to be run is essential. Rules vary from country to country, and even within a country. In England, for example, there are separate regulations for official Horse Trials, Hunter Trials, Pony Club and Riding Club Events. The course designer has to follow the rules relating to the height and width of obstacles, number of obstacles, the distance of the course, and the speed to be used.

Some rule books define a maximum number of drop fences, combinations, and jumping efforts. Though these rules may be regarded as a restriction on the course designer, they should be adhered to, as they were devised to protect the horse.

□In laying out the courses for a Three-Day Event there are many special requirements — in particular finding a suitable site for the Steeplechase, and mapping out the Roads and Tracks. Again, the going, the terrain available, and the distances required will be the primary considerations.

The Trout Hatchery at Burghley, a natural-looking water obstacle. However, an upright post and rail fence as the first element is not to be recommended. A horse's eye will be taken by the water beyond, so he may misjudge the height of the rail and hit it hard; also, being unsure of the depth of water, he will be reluctant to jump very high, making this an extremely difficult fence to jump into water. A solid, rounded log, as used for the 'out' is ideal.

Lucinda Green on Regal Realm, taking the three elements of the Burghley Coffin. Although the dimensions are formidable, the banks are not steep, and the distances—which allow one stride between each obstacle—are fair. The natural ditch has been enlarged and revetted on the take-off side.

(e) Siting the Fences

When the probable route has been determined, start to design the obstacles, by choosing where to put 'key' fences such as combinations, water obstacles and any other which uses important natural features on the site. After this, plan to use as many existing natural obstacles as possible, such as hedges, ditches, or other suitable boundaries. Having sketched a preliminary plan, ask yourself whether you have achieved a satisfactory balance in these obstacles.

The difficulty may be in providing variety among the more straightforward fences. First, decide what the obstacle will be — a spread or an upright — then choose the materials you will use for constructing it. A variation of materials used on a course is not a prime consideration, but it may add interest.

One of the hallmarks of good course design is the use of the right materials in the right place. For example, a pile of tyres will look ridiculous in the middle of a field, but it might be appropriate near a machinery shed by a farmyard. Stacks of cordwood or logpiles will look best close to a wood or a group of trees; and a water trough's natural position would be in a field boundary line, as though it were being used by animals.

As far as possible, you should try to use local materials. In some cases you may have to bring in timber from elsewhere, but it will probably look out of place. It is an accepted fact that the very best cross-country courses have a 'natural' look — though, of course, many of the fences will have been specifically created for the competition. Apart from cutting timber from woods on the site you are using, the best source is the nearest sawmill, where inevitably the timber will be local in origin.

☐ Grouping some obstacles together suits both spectators and television cameras. The FEI suggests that there should be four fences per kilometre on a cross-country course, but this is not essential and need not be followed too rigidly. Though it would be foolish to construct a course consisting of, for example, four groups of six fences (total 24 fences), with long gallops between each group, to build 24 separate fences with a 250-metre (270-yard) space between each would be very boring for spectators and, to some extent, for competitors.

☐ Most competitions have a number of different classes, and for each one the difficulty of the course taken as a whole must be relevant to the particular standard of horses and riders taking part. It will not be satisfactory simply to raise some fences in order to increase their difficulty; for example, an obstacle raised by 3 in (7 to 8 cm) is often barely more difficult, and would not test a higher grade of horse. Neither it is satisfactory to use a loop of additional fences to lengthen a course for a higher grade of competition if, as often happens, these may be the only fences which differentiate between one class and another. As an example, a Novice course of 20 fences does not become an Intermediate course by the addition of five or six individually difficult fences on a loop halfway round the course. A course must be of consistent standard throughout its length. At least two-thirds of the fences on a One-Day Event course should be individual to a particular class (i.e. not shared with other classes). At Hunter Trials, half the course ought to be separate. For a Three-Day Event there should be virtually 100 per cent difference between two levels of competition.

The easiest way to achieve the desired standard is to plan first the longer (or longest) of the courses to be built. It is nearly always easier to produce a satisfactory result by shortening a course for a lower grade than by lengthening a course to go up a grade.

☐ Course designers inevitably spend a lot of time dreaming up new obstacles. While ideas thought up in the bath can be extremely useful, it is seldom wise to imagine the fences and then go out on the site to try and find somewhere to put them!

Though a course must be consistent, every fence does not have to be of exactly the same degree of difficulty. It is advisable to follow a relatively dificult fence — whether it tests the horse's jumping ability, agility or accuracy — with something less demanding or rather different. The horse is then encouraged after a particular problem, rather than being confronted by the same problem at a series of obstacles closely following each other. In particular you should avoid having a succession of big drop fences, or two or three combinations in a row, or indeed several big spread fences one after the other, with no uprights or other kinds of fence in between. Generally, the 'easy' fences should be of maximum height and spread but should be built on relatively simple terrain.

☐ Finally, in considering the design and layout of a cross-country course it must be remembered that it is the terrain that distinguishes cross-country from show jumping, and it is the imaginative use of this terrain which is the hallmark of a good course designer. It is also the terrain that makes a fence difficult. No horse worth his salt will have the slightest problem jumping an obstacle of maximum height or spread if it is on flat ground and off a straight approach, but he could be in difficulty at a similar, much smaller fence, awkwardly placed.

Designing
the Obstacles

The following are the main points to be considered when designing a course:

1. What is the object of the course as a whole?
   (a) Is it an educational step for horse and/or rider?
   (b) Is it to test the best? If so, will the *worst* get round safely, or at least have some fun?
   (c) Is it difficult or easy enough for the horses and riders who are expected to jump it? In a Horse Trial or Three-Day Event, will it have the right influence on the overall competition, bearing in mind that the competition also includes dressage and show jumping phases?

2. Competition courses should always be designed to test progress, even at lower levels. Thus they may be educational for horses and riders progressing through the grades, but they are *not* intended to be schooling grounds.

3. You must comply implicitly with the relevant rules.

4. Always consider *why* you are using a particular fence. Possible reasons include:
   (a) To provide a warm-up for the rest of the course.
   (b) To use a natural hedge/fence line or feature.
   (c) To add variety to the course.
   (d) To test the horse's boldness.
   (e) To test the horse's agility. (But make sure that the fence is safe.)
   (f) To test the rider's ability. (But if he is inexperienced, is the fence safe?)
   (g) To provide a 'let up' after a difficult fence.
   (h) To provide interest for spectators. If so, it must also fulfil a purpose for horse and rider.

5. Consider *how* a *good* horse will jump the fence.
Is it comfortable for him?
Is it safe for the less able horse and rider?
It must be possible for *all* fences to be jumped in a fluent and attractive manner by the horse who is correctly presented at it and

has the necessary ability. Too often a course designer has no clear idea of what he expects a good horse to do at an obstacle. This applies particularly to combination fences, which should look quite simple when jumped well by the most able competitors.

6. Plan as much variety as possible within the course:
  (a) Use a variety of materials.
  (b) Use varying types of obstacle:
    Verticals (posts and rails, and filled, solid obstacles)
    Parallels (oxers)
    Ascending spreads
    Ditches: In front of a fence
            Under a fence
            Behind a fence
    Brush fences/hedges
    Steps up and down
    Banks
    Drops
    Water
    Tables

NB Make sure that the materials and the position of the obstacle blend as naturally as possible with the surrounding countryside.

7. Try to *balance* combinations and complexes with more straightforward 'galloping' obstacles. All courses need both. Horses should not be asked to gallop on a long stride for, say, half of the course, and then be asked to compress themselves and be very agile on the second half. The various qualities expected of them should be tested at intervals all round the course. This will also be more interesting for the spectator.

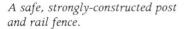
A safe, strongly-constructed post and rail fence.

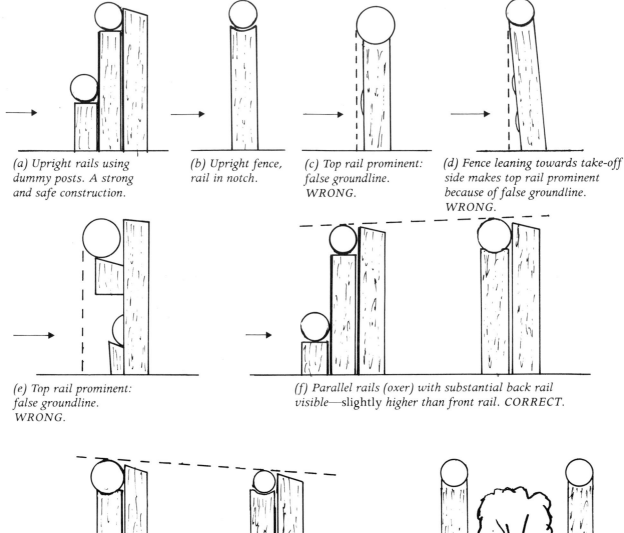

(a) Upright rails using dummy posts. A strong and safe construction.

(b) Upright fence, rail in notch.

(c) Top rail prominent: false groundline. WRONG.

(d) Fence leaning towards take-off side makes top rail prominent because of false groundline. WRONG.

(e) Top rail prominent: false groundline. WRONG.

(f) Parallel rails (oxer) with substantial back rail visible—slightly *higher* than front rail. CORRECT.

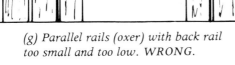

(g) Parallel rails (oxer) with back rail too small and too low. WRONG.

(h) Oxer with false groundline: top rail more prominent than base of hedge. WRONG.

8. The course must be consistent. A course within which the standard of difficulty varies too much is unsatisfactory.

9. CORRECT BALANCE OF EASY/DIFFICULT OBSTACLES
In principle, all courses should be broken down into easy (or straightforward) and more difficult sections. Two, three, or even

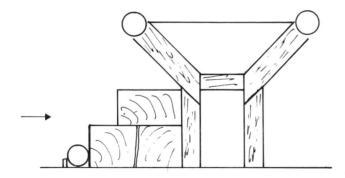

(i) Hayrack with groundline.

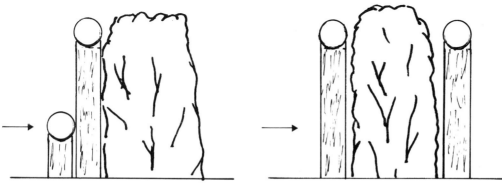

(j) Oxer with rails before hedge.
SAFE.

(k) Oxer with back rail not visible.
UNSAFE.

four testing obstacles may be grouped together or may succeed one another — but they must be followed by one or two straightforward fences.

A straightforward or 'let up' fence should look solid and inviting, and probably should be sited on fairly flat ground. However, it can be of maximum size.

10. WHAT MAKES AN OBSTACLE EASY OR DIFFICULT?

At all levels it is the terrain, or the grouping of fences, which makes an obstacle easy or difficult. Size is *relatively* unimportant, particularly on flat ground. This is the greatest difference between cross-country and show jumping.

An ascending spread on flat ground is the easiest type of fence to jump, for the following reasons:

(a) The shape of the fence makes it comparatively easy for both horse and rider to judge the appropriate take-off point. Even if one or both of them gets it wrong it is unlikely to matter much. Should the horse stand off too far, a long arc will probably carry him over the spread. It is almost impossible to get too close to such a fence.

(b) The speed of the approach to the obstacle is relatively unimport- ant. Because of the limited heights of cross-country obstacles, any competent horse will jump such obstacles whether he is trotting or galloping.

(c) No great accuracy is required on the part of the rider or of the horse. They can jump the fence at any place between the flags, and can approach from almost any direction.

(d) Such a fence does not test the horse's boldness; he can clearly see what he has to do and where he is going; there is no ditch or water which could frighten him; and unless the fence is made of startling material he will negotiate it with confidence.

(e) No other fence is related to this obstacle, so the horse is not required to show his agility, manoeuvrability or obedience, either in the approach or on landing.

(f) The rider is not required to make any choice or important decision as to how to negotiate the obstacle.

Having considered the easiest type of fence it may now be appropriate to analyse the factors that make up a more difficult one:

(a) The need for a correct take-off point becomes more important when the fence is either a vertical, a big spread, or — at the extreme — a parallel bar. In the case of a true vertical, horses can easily get too close, hit the fence hard, and possibly fall. With a big spread, if the horse stands back too far he may not clear the back of the fence.

(b) The speed of the approach becomes important when an obstacle involves a drop, a landing into water, a combination fence, a complex of related fences, or a turn either into or away from the obstacles.

(c) Accuracy will be tested when a fence is narrow, on an angle, or on a slope. It is particularly important at combination fences. A course designer must be careful that in testing accuracy he does not trap a horse. He must also consider what might happen when the rider lacks judgement: if the result is a bad fall, the fence is not suitable.

(d) Boldness will be important when, for example, the horse must jump from light into dark (which often causes trouble); or 'into space' where the horse cannot see the landing; or into water; or into what appears to be a confined space, such as a farmyard; or when there is a ditch on the take-off side or underneath the fence.

(e) The agility of the horse will be tested at steps, banks, uphill fences, combinations or related obstacles. An extreme example is a bounce — two obstacles without a non-jumping stride between them.

(f) The rider is forced to take decisions and to make choices through the use of options, alternatives and combinations (as described by Neil Ayer in this book). Again, it is the course designer's task to avoid the risk of bad falls for horses whose riders are incompetent.

Although the actual dimensions of a fence will be important in certain situations, the height and spread are the least important factors in making a fence more, or less, difficult.

☐ The most difficult fence of all is one which incorporates virtually all of the factors listed above, and the art of the course designer is to decide which factors to incorporate into a particular obstacle. When he uses several types of test at one fence he will have to adjust the height of the obstacle accordingly: for example if there is a fence into water which tests the speed of the approach and the boldness of the horse, the obstacle should be much lower than one built on flat ground. Though a designer is generally guided by the rules which specify height and spread for the relevant standard of competition, he should never decide on the exact dimensions of an obstacle before its construction is more or less completed. Only then will he be able to assess it accurately and to adjust it to the appropriate size — ensuring that it presents the correct degree of difficulty for the competition.

☐ The exact position of a particular fence in relation to the site on which it is built will often determine the degree of difficulty. The diagram shows a vertical obstacle positioned in three alternative places on a slope. *Position 1*, right on the edge of a downhill slope, is the most difficult because it has an 'into space' effect and tests the horse's boldness and agility simultaneously. *Position 2* may test his boldness because the landing platform might seem short and he cannot see exactly where he is going to land; but it does not involve a drop and is therefore easier than Position 1. *Position 3* is the easiest of all for a horse to jump, as he can see where he is going, and the landing and take-off are in the same plane.

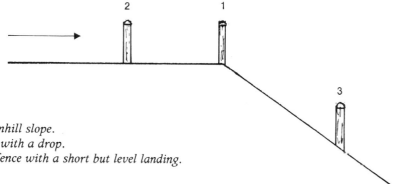

Easy/difficult fences
Choice of position for a fence on a downhill slope.
(1) DIFFICULT *Level approach to a fence with a drop.*
(2) LESS DIFFICULT *Level approach to a fence with a short but level landing.*
(3) EASY *Downhill approach with drop.*

11. THE DIFFERENCE BETWEEN DIFFICULT AND DANGEROUS OBSTACLES.

All course designers will want to include difficult obstacles on the course, to test the horses' and riders' ability. However, dangerous obstacles must be avoided at all times and it is therefore necessary to consider what will happen to a horse that does not negotiate an obstacle correctly. If a fall is *likely*, the fence is dangerous, but sometimes falls occur because of riders' or horses' errors.

☐ A notorious example of a dangerous obstacle was Fence 2 in the 1973 European Championships at Kiev. It consisted of wide parallel bars over a ditch, with a downhill approach off a turn. The riders found it almost impossible to generate enough impulsion from their horses to clear the obstacle, and far too many of them landed short — in the middle of the parallel.

☐ An example of a very difficult fence was the famous Serpent (No. 23) at the 1978 World Championships in Lexington. The many falls and stops at this fence were brought about by a combination of tricky terrain, a take-off that became mushy through splashing, and oppressive, airless heat. A difficult fence such as this, which tests riders and horses in several ways, may become impossible when weather conditions change and if the going deteriorates during the course of a competition.

Notes on the Siting and Design of the Principal Types of Obstacle

FENCES ON HILLS AND SLOPES. Vertical or slightly sloping fences are recommended for this type of terrain.

Uphill Try not to build fences on uphill slopes. Even if measured correctly they will look small and jump badly.

Fences can be usefully sited just over the top or brow of a hill. Or steps can be cut into a hill.

Downhill Fences on downhill slopes look impressively big but they jump relatively easily. They can be sited:

    (a) At the top of a slope. This is a test of boldness.

    (b) On a slope. This tests control and balance.

    (c) At the bottom or just after the bottom of a slope. This tests agility.

The impact of jumping on to sloping ground Though it is not physically taxing for a horse to land on a downhill slope, it can cause him to leave his hind legs and can also damage his back. It should therefore be avoided.

FENCES AT THE BOTTOM OF SLOPES. *Position a* is the most difficult for a horse to jump, as he will have to take off from the short bit of flat ground in front of the obstacle and it is not easy to judge or control each stride coming down the slope in front of the fence.

Position b is easier than *a* because the take-off point is less critical, but it involves a drop.

Position c in which the horse has a full stride on level ground before jumping the obstacle, is obviously the easiest.

An example of a very demanding obstacle sited in *Position a* was Fence 2 at the Montreal Olympics. This was a ditch and rails forming a spread, and it was particularly difficult for horses to produce enough impulsion after having virtually slid down the very steep slope in front of the fence.

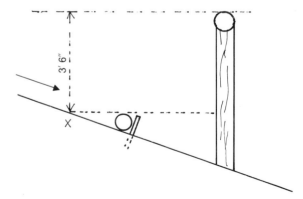

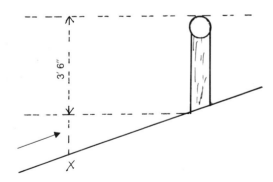

Measurement
*(a) Downhill fence which measures
3 ft 6 ins (1.06 m) at take-off point: X.
Note guard rail.*

*(b) AVOID BUILDING A FENCE ON AN UPHILL
SLOPE.*
*Uphill fence of 3 ft 6 ins (1.06 m) but much higher from
take-off point: X. Therefore illegal.*

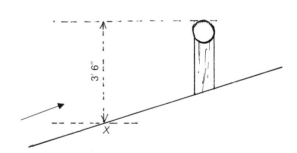

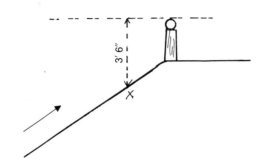

*(c) Uphill fence of 3 ft 6 ins (1.06 m) at take-off point:
X. Correct, but looks very under-sized.*

*(d) Small fence on top of steep hill (3 ft 6 in or 1.06 m
from take-off). A fair test.*

Bottom of slope
(a) DIFFICULT *Very cramped take-off area, after hazardous approach.*
(b) LESS DIFFICULT *Take-off from the bank.*
(c) EASY *Room to recover from descent before jumping off level ground.*

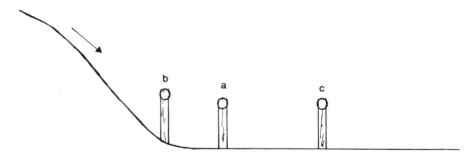

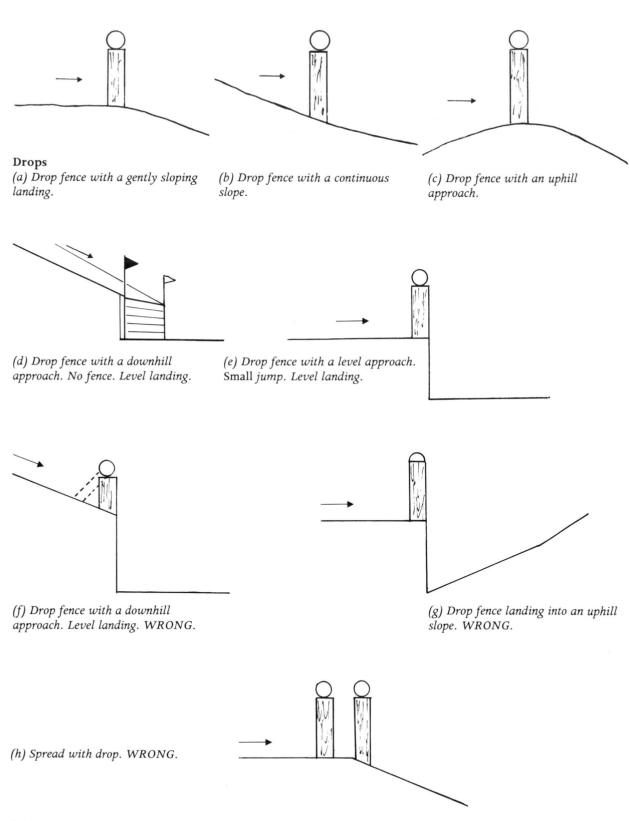

Drops

(a) Drop fence with a gently sloping landing.

(b) Drop fence with a continuous slope.

(c) Drop fence with an uphill approach.

(d) Drop fence with a downhill approach. No fence. Level landing.

(e) Drop fence with a level approach. Small jump. Level landing.

(f) Drop fence with a downhill approach. Level landing. WRONG.

(g) Drop fence landing into an uphill slope. WRONG.

(h) Spread with drop. WRONG.

DROP FENCES. Nearly all courses include some drop fences. They can be a legitimate test of a horse's balance, boldness and agility, but the wrong type of drop, or too many drops, are liable to damage horses' legs and also their confidence.

On some sites the inclusion of drops is unavoidable, such as when adjacent fields are on different levels.

The kindest type of drop is where the horse lands on ground that is sloping gently downhill.

Drops on to flat ground will always cause some jarring to a horse's legs and feet.

Drops on to rising ground (reverse slopes) should *never* be used on a course.

It is almost impossible to specify the maximum percentage of drops to be used on a particular course. However, several drop fences in succession should always be avoided. Three in a row, for example, would be too many — except perhaps in a downhill combination.

Jumping off a bank or down steps involves a drop — usually on to flat ground. Preferably this should be followed by a fence on the flat.

A big spread with a drop is particularly dangerous and should be avoided: horses are likely to hit it very hard. When a horse realises that he is approaching a drop fence he prepares himself for a lower landing, and his natural tendency is to minimise the drop by lowering his 'undercarriage' as soon as possible. When the drop fence is also a spread, such as a parallel (oxer), he may therefore land on the back of the fence or drop short between the rails, with disastrous consequences.

Small spread fences with a drop are perfectly acceptable, but maximum effort should not be demanded.

COFFINS. The degree of difficulty of a coffin is dictated by the steepness of the slope on either side of the ditch and by the closeness or otherwise of the rails to the ditch. It is a classic fence which usefully tests a horse's boldness and agility and a rider's ability to approach it at the correct speed. It must always be used with great discretion if it is not to sap the confidence of horse and rider.

The easiest version of a coffin will be on almost level ground, with an encouraging low first element and allowing at least one full stride before the ditch. The further away the rails from the ditch, the easier the fence will be, but it is the steepness of the slope that is more important. A difficult coffin with a high and upright first and/or last element and steeply sloping sides must clearly allow for the horse to take a stride between each part.

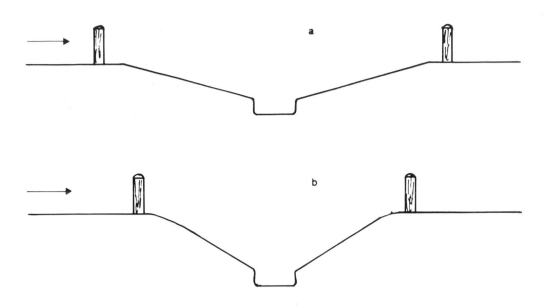

Coffins

(a) EASY *Almost level banks, good vision. Preferably one stride between each element.*

(b) DIFFICULT *Steep banks. Fore-shortened view from take-off requires advanced training and athletic ability.*

Parallels on a downhill slope.
(a) WRONG. Back pole too low.
(b) CORRECT, but avoid wide spread.

SPREAD FENCES. The parallel bar is the most difficult spread fence for both horse and rider. It requires a fairly accurate take-off position and a strong approach, full of impulsion, to carry the horse over the spread. If the parallel has a true vertical face to it, horses which get too close may hit the front rails with their forelegs and possibly may fall.

NB. Spread fences should not be sited on either uphill or downhill slopes.

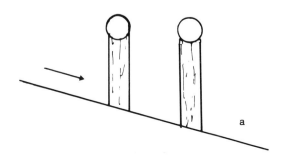

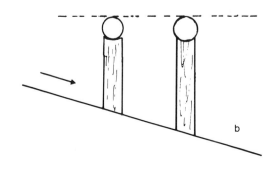

BOUNCE FENCES. The bounce is a very useful obstacle for testing a horse's agility and a rider's ability to judge pace. However, it should rarely be used at Horse Trials below Intermediate level. If it is included at Novice level (Preliminary in the United States) a suitable alternative route should always be provided. The course designer may offer the option of a bounce as an educational opportunity for horse and rider but should be confident that only those riders whose horses are ready for it will tackle the bounce.

DITCHES. There are three possible positions for a ditch in relation to a hedge, rails, or other form of obstacle. The easiest type of ditch to jump is the one which lies directly beneath the fence, with the fence itself providing a good take-off, and to some extent obscuring the ditch. The most difficult type is where the whole of the ditch lies in front of the fence, thus presenting a gaping hole to the horse, and also a maximum or near maximum spread.

Ditches can, of course, be made even more difficult by incorporating other tests such as accuracy. For example, a zig-zag over a ditch which has to be jumped on an angle over a narrow part of the fence will require precise riding.

A ditch on the landing side of a fence is only a test to a horse if he can actually see it. A 'blind' ditch on the landing side is therefore pointless, and the only possible influence that it will have on the competition is causing a horse to fall because he did not jump far enough out. This is in principle an unfair test, as the horse could not reasonably be expected to know that he should jump so far out. Whenever possible, ditches on the landing side of fences should be visible. If they are not, they should be narrow enough to ensure that any competent horse will clear them.

Ditches
(a) EASY *Ditch is below sloping rails, therefore incidental.*
(b) DIFFICULT *Ditch is wide and most significant. Horse must jump* high *as well as wide to clear far rails.*

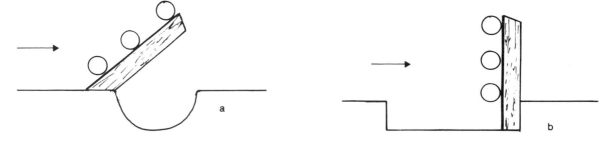

WATER. To test a horse's boldness, water need not be more than 3 to 4 inches (8 to 10 cm) deep. At all Events except those of the highest international level, water should be kept shallow. The use of deeper water at major competitions is for testing the rider's ability to approach it at the correct speed — i.e. slowly enough to land safely yet not so slowly that the horse will refuse to jump into it. This is a perfectly legitimate test, but it should be used only at the very top level.

Spread into water

UNFAIR *Horses may lower their hind legs quickly, coming down hard on the back of the spread, and possibly falling.*

ANGLED FENCES. The course designer must not ask a horse to jump a fence at too acute an angle. Falls at an angled fence are very common because it is easy to misjudge it, hit it obliquely, and lose balance. While the use of angles is an accepted test of both horse and rider, the designer must ensure that there is a safe — and possibly longer — approach which allows the fence to be jumped straight.

CORNERS. The principal function of corners is to test the rider's ability to present his horse with accuracy and the horse's willingness to hold a true line over a fence. By their very nature, corners invite the less obedient horse to run out at the side of the fence. The degree of difficulty will depend on whether or not the fence has a wing, how wide the angle makes it, and its exact siting.

The line of approach to a corner fence is very important. If it forms part of a combination, the designer must be absolutely certain that the rider can still find a true straight line across it. In combinations, a corner should always be positioned so that there is a true stride between it and another part of the obstacle.

The most difficult and uncomfortable corners are those on a twisty woodland track, where no rhythm can be established.

TURNS. Obviously, the more gentle a turn the easier it is for a horse to negotiate. Young and experienced horses and novice riders should not be asked to negotiate tight turns at speed.

The most difficult bends for horse and rider are 'S bends' — where it is not easy to keep a horse balanced.

Several fences in a straight line are also taxing. When a horse is asked to gallop straight for too long, his attention wanders and he tends to waver off line.

When sharp turns have to be incorporated in a course they are easier and less disruptive to the 'flow' if they come shortly before or after an obstacle. At such points a rider should be collecting and balancing his horse.

Avoid turns on ground which slopes away downwards. If unbalanced, the horse will be liable to slip.

The Ideal Course

The ideal course should start on flat ground, with a run of approximately 50 metres (55 yards) to the first fence. It should be on a slight curve, which will make it easier for the rider to control and balance his horse. This first fence should be an ascending spread, which is the easiest obstacle of all. It should be about 10% below maximum height and about 50% of the maximum spread, but will be solid and will encourage horses to jump fluently and big.

The next two obstacles should be massive in appearance, still on relatively flat ground, with no technical problem. They may incorporate a small ditch, a big spread or a slight slope. The height of these fences can be at, or near to, the maximum allowed for the class.

Depending on the total number of obstacles on the course, the first combination or complex of fences should appear between a quarter and a third of the way round.

The middle third of the course should be the most difficult. The last quarter should be more difficult than the first quarter. Water obstacles, if included, should be in the middle third.

The last fence should be as big as reasonably possible, but uncomplicated. Riders must *not* be encouraged to gallop flat out for the finish.

Bad courses are inconsistent, trappy, tricky, flimsy. They penalise bold horses, or include fences which ask contradictory questions.

An extreme example of the latter is a big spread into water. The spread invites a galloping approach, yet riders should jump as slowly as they dare into water; it has a considerably dragging effect on the horse, and too fast an entry is liable to cause a fall.

Final Thoughts

Course designers always walk a tightrope. If the course is too easy, many competitors will be happy, but the best won't necessarily win and the competition will be dull. If it is too difficult, the designer will be regarded as a sadistic idiot!

You will never please all the riders all the time. Attempt to do so and you will end up with the lowest common denominator.

Be bold. But always ask yourself:

Why am I doing *this*?

How will they jump *this*?

How can I improve it next time?

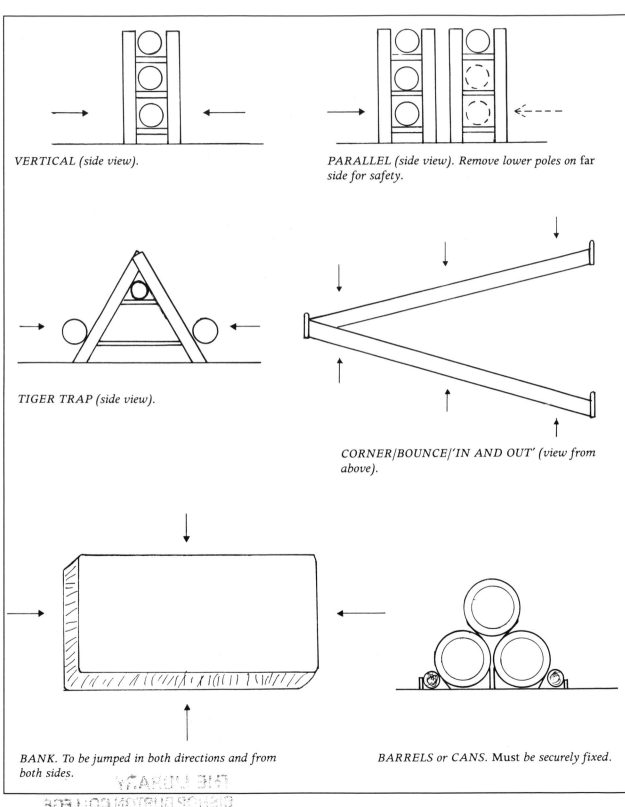

VERTICAL (side view).

PARALLEL (side view). Remove lower poles on far side for safety.

TIGER TRAP (side view).

CORNER/BOUNCE/'IN AND OUT' (view from above).

BANK. To be jumped in both directions and from both sides.

BARRELS or CANS. Must be securely fixed.

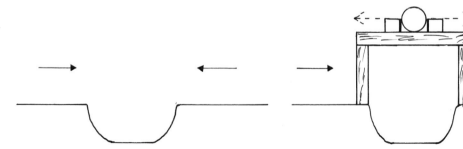

DITCH (OPEN). Do not revet banks unless only jumped one way, when take-off may be strengthened. Banks should be sound and well-defined.

DITCH WITH RAIL (TRAKEHNER). The rail may be moved to front or back of ditch, to alter difficulty, or angled across. Secure firmly with blocks.

Schooling Fences

The more solid the fence, the better it will survive, the safer it will be, and the better the horse will jump it.

A good groundline is most important. Do not make gaps, i.e. 3 in to 8 in (8 cm to 20 cm) which could trap a horse's foot.

Avoid:
Straw Bales. They break up, rot, or move, and horses tend not to respect them because they lack a solid appearance. If you do use them, always reinforce them with rails.
Hurdles. They tend to break easily, as does any wood which snaps or splinters when struck.
Metal Cans. They rust, and if trodden upon jagged edges may appear. Beware of **nails** and other sharp protrusions which could injure horse or rider.

'Portable' Obstacles

When a cross-country site is temporary, of if a course has to be dismantled after use, it is practical and more economical to use some portable fences. These may also prove useful when several competitions are held in the same place, to vary the course and to avoid patches of poached or bare ground.

Note that a simple fence can become considerably more difficult when positioned at a different angle, or on or near a slope, or close to another obstacle.

Typical examples of portable fences:

Brush, or birch fence, in a frame.

Seat.

Table-type fence.

Palisade.

Hayrack.

Important

If a fence is light enough to be 'portable' it is not likely to be heavy or stable enough to remain fixed in place when a horse hits it. To make it safe it must be secured to the ground, so that it cannot shift.

Constructing the Obstacles

1. SOME GENERAL POINTS

☐ Before you start to build a cross-country course, cost will obviously be an important consideration. Make sure that you are going to have enough money to build the whole course to a satisfactory standard. It would be a shame to have half a course well built with good solid timber and the other half 'bodged' up by using flimsy second-hand timber because the finances have run out. If money *is* short you should economise on alternatives, dressing, and other non-essential detail — not on the basic materials.

☐ Careful planning can save you time and money. If you are not sure about something, call in expert advice. This could save you having to make unnecessary changes later.

☐ As well as having the correct influence on the competition, every cross-country fence should be safe, strong, and attractive to look at. Of these considerations, safety is the most important.

☐ An obstacle must have a sound take-off and landing; soft or badly poached ground around it causes a horse unnecessary stress or strain when he jumps.

☐ Fences should be constructed so that they minimise any injury to a horse should he hit the fence hard or become trapped in it. Prominent edges of timber should be rounded off, and any sharp metal fixings covered over or avoided altogether. Avoid gaps between timbers just wide enough (4 in to 12 in, 10 cm to 30 cm) for a horse to put his foot through. If his leg drops into a narrow gap while travelling forward at speed or becomes trapped between the rails when refusing to jump, the horse can be seriously injured.

The front and top of the fence should either be solid and strong enough to support a horse's weight if he should jump against it or on to the top of it, or the timbers should be far enough apart to ensure that if a horse's leg goes between them it can come out again with plenty of room to spare. It is best to use strong rope to keep the top rails in position. Then, if a horse should become trapped, anyone with a sharp penknife can cut the ropes quickly and lower the rail to the ground so that the horse can be extricated before any harm is done.

☐ Where solid timbers are combined with brush or hedge-type obstacles the solid part of the fence must *always* be clearly visible to the horse. If a rail is hidden out of sight in the top of a hedge fence it can cause a nasty fall when a horse brushes through the top of it and hits the rail which he did not know was there.

☐ When you are building an obstacle over or in the line of a wire stock-fence, the wire should be completely covered over between the boundary flags of the fence, and guard rails should be placed along the top of the wire at least 12 ft (3.5 m) either side. Whenever you finish building a fence, stand back, look at it, and ask yourself whether there is anything on or around it which could in any way be dangerous. You may well save yourself from being sent back to correct the fence by the Course Inspection Steward or the Technical Delegate.

☐ Fences should be built strongly, so that they will not in any way be damaged or altered in appearance by horses jumping them. They should be firm enough to withstand many heavy knocks. Uprights should be set firmly in the ground, so that they are immovable. Ideally they should not be more than 8 ft to 10 ft (2.5 m to 3 m) apart; if the design of the fence is such that they have to be wider apart, the posts may need some form of extra support. Any portable fence should be securely anchored to the ground with stakes, so that a horse refusing the fence and hitting it with his chest cannot move it.

A strong, well-constructed fence, seen from the landing side.

For the same reason, logs or tree trunks should also be fixed securely. *A solidly built fence will be a good investment as it will jump better and last longer than a weaker one.*

☐ Fences should be as wide as possible so that horses do not always take off and land on the same patches of ground. A narrow fence, as well as being less inviting to jump, can become hazardous after heavy rainfall, when a horse cannot avoid the areas of badly poached or slippery ground on either side of it. If your budget will not allow the ideal width of fence, then any island fences you build will almost certainly need wings.

☐ Try to get local firms to sponsor fences, and shop around for your materials, but beware of buying anything unseen.

☐ Voluntary labour is obviously an attractive way of reducing costs, but steer clear of over-enthusiastic volunteers who when unsupervised make mistakes which are expensive to remedy. A party of Pony Club children let loose with creosote and brushes can put an awful lot of creosote on the ground and very little on the fences!

☐ Try to make your fences as varied and attractive in appearance as possible. If your site has several natural fences, such as hedges which all look the same, there is no point in removing them and building something else in their place; it is always possible to dress them up in different ways. Ideally, try not to have more than one fence of a particular type. If a course is repetitive it may become boring for competitors and spectators.

☐ Smart timber will help to make a fence look attractive, especially if it is all of the same type — either all rustic with the bark on, or all peeled with the bark removed and the poles tidily creosoted. When it is not possible to use the same timber on the whole course, or if more variety is required, you can use different types for different fences. Try to make it 'fit in' with its natural surroundings as far as possible. Use the minimum number of rope and wire fixings, and keep these neat and tidy. Cut off any excess pieces of timber flush with the edges of the fence and then rasp the cut edges to remove any whiskers left by the saw and to make the edges less sharp if a horse should hit them.

The look of a fence can be improved by the addition of spruce branches used for infilling underneath the top rail, and Christmas trees can be temporarily planted on either side of the fence as wings. Birch can be used in the same way. You can also put boxes of flowers, or pots of shrubs underneath fences to smarten their appearance.

☐ Alternative fences obviously give the course builder more scope for imagination, but there is no point in building them unless all the options incorporated in the fence are going to be jumped in the competition. The most difficult option must be on the quickest route, and unless the easier options take much longer to negotiate there is no point in competitors trying the more difficult route.

☐ Because cross-country fences are measured from a point where a horse will take off, fences built on an uphill slope will always tend to look small, often surprisingly so, particularly if they have a spread.

Fences built on a downhill slope can be made to look extremely large.
□Before starting to build a fence, time spent looking round for the best piece of ground on which to put it is never wasted. If you cannot visualise what a fence is going to look like, knock in some light stakes where the posts are going to be. This will help you to get the proportions of the fence right, particularly in the case of combinations. Beware of setting up a top rail of smaller diameter than the one which you eventually intend to use, as this can give you a misleading impression of how the finished fence will look. First, position the uprights correctly, then offer up the rail which will be there permanently, then adjust it to the correct height.

With these basic principles in mind, you should be ready to start putting fences together.

2. LABOUR, EQUIPMENT AND TIMBER

LABOUR

A course builder needs to be a cross between a carpenter, a forester, an agricultural fencing man, and a groundwork contractor. A knowledge of horses and their capabilities is also a great advantage, but it is not essential if the builder is advised by an experienced designer. It is possible for one man on his own to build fences, if he has the necessary skill, the mechanical aids, and plenty of time and energy. There will, however, be some jobs with which he will need assistance. The ideal number of men for building cross-country courses is probably two — so that, for example, while one drives the tractor, the other can give directions, or while one holds a pole in position the other stands back to see if it is in the right place. A team of three men can also work well together, but will not necessarily do the same amount of work three times as quickly. If more than three are available, they should be split into two teams as long as there are enough tools and equipment to go round. If one person is standing around waiting for another to do something, they will get in each other's way, which is time-wasting.

Building a fence can take anything from half a day to a week. Earthworks and water fences can take even longer. Timber-type fences above ground-level can be constructed as near to the time of the competition as you like, as long as enough time is allowed for the course to be inspected and for any subsequent alterations to be carried out. If the fences are built too long before the competition they may look 'weathered' before they are used, or they may be damaged by livestock walking round the fences and wearing away the ground, rubbing against the fences, or pulling the bark off the poles. However, any work which involves moving earth or turf should be undertaken up to a year in advance and then fenced off to protect the area from livestock. Banks and steps can be constructed nearer to the time of the Event as long as they are back-filled with stone (see page 132).

Fence builders at work.

ESSENTIAL EQUIPMENT

The amateur, part-time, or weekend course builder will not want to invest large sums of money on elaborate tools and machinery, but certain items of equipment are essential for completing the job easily and quickly.

(a) Vehicles

Every course builder must have a suitable type of vehicle, which can transport heavy timber round the course and carry the necessary tools. A four-wheel drive vehicle, such as a Land-Rover, is ideal because it can tow a low-loading trailer and will cope easily with wet and uneven ground.

The average private car is inadequate for heavy duty work and could be damaged. Also if you spin the wheels of your vehicle or get it stuck on the course — or, even worse, in front of a fence — it can leave an ugly mess.

Although you may be able to carry short lengths of timber on your vehicle, remember that long poles are very heavy and can be difficult to lift — on to roof racks for instance. If you drag timber about, it not only damages the ground but also the timber itself, and ropes and chains will wear out. A tractor pulling a trailer is one

51

*A low-loading, flat, open trailer,
ideal for carrying fence materials.*

solution, but it is slow, and in rainy conditions all the equipment will get wet, and metals, such as nails, will rust. A four-wheel drive towing a low-loading trailer is preferable. Make sure that the trailer's wheels are far enough back from the tow hitch so that when long poles are carried they are equally balanced fore and aft: if they overhang the back of the trailer too much, their weight will tend to lift up the rear of the towing vehicle. On a public road this could be extremely dangerous as it could cause the vehicle and trailer to snake or perhaps to jack-knife. Similarly, poles overhanging the front of the trailer too much could foul the rear of the towing vehicle when turning sharply.

For certain tasks, a tractor fitted with a fore-end loader is invaluable. This can be used for lifting and positioning heavy poles and also for pulling posts out of the ground. A bucket fitted to the arms will load or move earth or stone. A medium-sized tractor with a post-hole borer or post-driver fitted to the back and a fore-end loader at the front is ideal, but remember that a fore-end loader will reduce the manoeuvrability of the tractor and make the steering heavier. You may also need some type of tipping trailer or dumper for moving earth and stone. For major digging operations, a back-hoe type digger can usually be hired quite easily by the hour or by the day.

(b) Machinery

A CHAINSAW is probably the course builder's most useful machine. It is sold in a wide variety of forms and sizes, but a good petrol-driven chainsaw with an engine size of 40–70 cc is the most practical version. If possible, use a 15 in-(40 cm-) long guide-bar, which is short enough to be manoeuvred easily when doing intricate carpentry yet is capable of cutting timber 30 in (80 cm) in diameter (it can cut down both sides of a log).

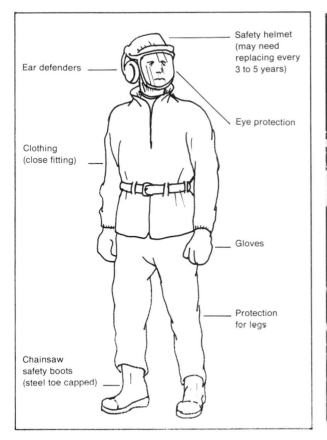

Safety helmet (may need replacing every 3 to 5 years)

Ear defenders

Eye protection

Clothing (close fitting)

Gloves

Protection for legs

Chainsaw safety boots (steel toe capped)

Above *Chainsaw in use. Note that protective clothing as seen on the left is now compulsory.*

IMPORTANT Make sure that you know how to use the chainsaw safely and efficiently. Before buying one, ask the advice of someone who is experienced. Though modern chainsaws have sophisticated safety devices built into them — a necessary precaution — they can be dangerous, even when used by a skilled operator.

Anyone operating a chainsaw is now required *by law* in the U.K. to wear special protective clothing. This will include tough, toe-capped boots, which are recommended at all times for course building, as it is very easy to drop a heavy piece of timber on your foot. Ordinary wellington boots afford little protection, and they (very annoyingly) tend to fill up with sawdust. It is also advisable to wear a safety helmet with ear-defenders and a visor to protect your eyes and face, and these are compulsory when using a chainsaw. Make sure you are acquainted with the current regulations!

It is possible to put small posts into the ground by hand. If you are strong and if conditions are easy, use a DRIVE-ALL (see page 54). This a steel tube about 3 ft (90 cm) long with a plate on one end and a handle on either side by which it is raised and lowered. It is only suitable for the building of small fences.

For heavy work a variety of machines is available to make the task easier. A POST-HOLE BORER DRIVEN BY A SMALL PETROL ENGINE has to be manoeuvred into position by hand. If the ground is stony, or if the

Drive-all.

Right *Post-driver (tractor-mounted).*

auger hits a root, the machine might easily become stuck and it will be very difficult to get it out of the ground again. This type of machine can only drill holes up to a certain diameter.

To operate any of the other machines you will need a tractor.

A POST-HOLE BORER MOUNTED ON A TRACTOR will bore wide enough holes for any cross-country course fence quickly and easily, but you still have to fill in the hole, and ram the earth tight round the post, by hand.

A POST-DRIVER MOUNTED ON A TRACTOR is probably the best tool for the job. It has a very heavy weight which is raised by the power take-off of the tractor then drops on to the top of the post and simply drives it very firmly into the ground, like a giant hammer.

As some of these machines are more efficient and easier to manoeuvre into position than others, choose one which is best suited to your particular requirements. All of them should be handled with great care.

Above *Post-hole borer (hand version).*

Above right *Removing a post with a tractor-mounted fore-end loader and chain.*

Right *Post-hole borer (tractor-mounted).*

Back-hoe digger.

(c) Tools
The following are indispensable:

CLAW HAMMER. A 20 oz (560 g) hammer is the most useful: preferably one with a steel or fibre glass shaft; wooden-shafted hammers will not last as long, particularly if they are used for pulling out nails.

FENCING PLIERS are very useful as they are so versatile. They will cut wire, hold wire while it is twisted, or, by using the spike, they can be driven under a staple (see illustration) to loosen it, then by taking hold of the staple with the pliers' jaw, it can be pulled out the rest of the way. Pliers can also be used to grip rope when you are pulling it up tight.

SPADE. Choose a spade of well-known make, which will be much more likely to stand up to hard wear and tear. It should have a deep, sharp edge.

CROWBAR. A 5 ft- (1.5 m) long crowbar with a point at one end and a chisel at the other is essential for levering rails off posts and for making pilot holes in the ground for stakes. You can manoeuvre surprisingly large pieces of timber by using the leverage afforded by a good crowbar.

JEMMY. This is a curved steel bar with a claw on one end and a chisel point on the other. Make sure that you have one which is long

Claw hammer and pliers used for raising a staple.

Below: Fence pliers used for removing a staple.

Collection of hand tools.
(1) 10 mm 3 m-long tow chain with hook and ring. (2) Turning lever. (3) Slasher. (4) Jemmy. (5) 3 kg sledgehammer. (6) Fencing mall. (7) 1.5 m crowbar. (8) Spade. (9) Short-handled shovel. (10) Long-handled Irish shovel. (11) High-lift jack. (12) Post-hole tamper. (13) Long-handled pruners. (14) Garden-type shears. (15) Shackles. (16) Timber-lifting tongs. (17) Penknife. (18) Carpenter's brace. (19) Auger bits. (20) Surform or rasp. (21) Hacksaw. (22) Fencing pliers. (23) Wire-cutting pliers. (24) Tommy bar. (25) Claw hammer. (26) Adjustable spanner. (27) Plumber's stilsons.

enough (at least 3 ft, or 90 cm) to give you enough leverage to pull out 6 in- (15 cm) nails from very hard timber.

SLEDGEHAMMER. If this is the only implement you have for driving stakes into the ground you will need quite a large one. Use it on its side so that the larger, flatter bit of the head hits the stake, as this will do less damage.

BOW SAW. This D-shaped saw has a thin blade which is suitable for cutting rustic timber.

TAPE-MEASURE. Two different sizes may be needed: (1) a pocket tape up to about 10 ft (3 m) long for measuring shorter lengths of timber, (2) a tape at least 49 ft to 66 ft (15 m to 20 m) long for accurately measuring the distance between elements of fences and for the longer lengths of timber. The best long tape-measure is called a *logger's tape*. It has a very sharp hook attached to the free end, which anchors it firmly in the timber; when the hook is released, a spring rewinds the tape, which saves a lot of time.

MEASURING STICK. If the fences you are building are subject to regulations, you will need a good measuring stick to make sure that the height and spread are the right size. The height of a cross-

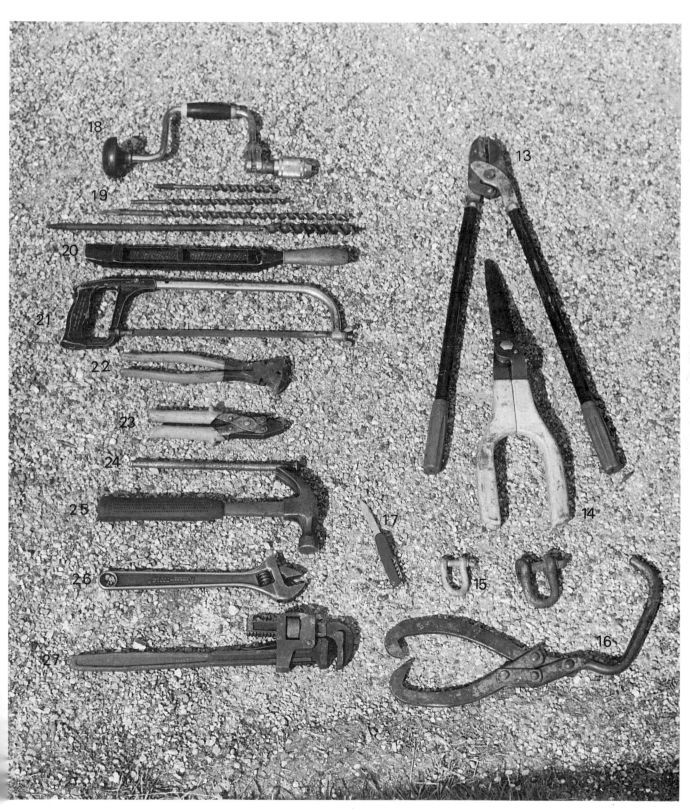

Measuring height, using forked props.

Surform used to smooth and level rough edges.

country fence is measured from a point where the average horse would normally be expected to take off. To do this, use a long, straight-edged bar with a spirit level fitted which will reach back from the top rail of the fence to above the point where the horse should take off. Adjust the horizontal stick until it is level, then measure from this spot down to the ground. You will then be able to determine the height/size of the fence. The most useful material for your level stick is aluminium channel, as used in making shelves. It is straight, strong, light and easy to carry about. Light pieces of wood tend to warp and twist, particularly if they have got wet and have been frequently carried around in a vehicle. You will need a surprisingly long stick to reach from where a horse will take off across a ditch to a rail on the far side, or across a fence which has a very large spread: on an Advanced course, for example, up to 9 ft 2 in (2.8 m). (See page 172.)

Other hand tools which, although not essential, will help to make course building easier, include:

LEVER ACTION WIRE OR BOLT CUTTERS. A pair of these, if of good quality, will cut wire more efficiently than fencing pliers. They will also cut through nails and thin pieces of steel and light chain.

SURFORM OR RASP. This is handy for removing any sharp edges and for putting finishing touches to your fences. Where you have cut a piece of timber, remove any sharp edges that the horse is likely to brush against.

TOMMY BAR. A bar 8 in to 10 in (20 cm to 25 cm) long and $\frac{3}{8}$ in to $\frac{1}{2}$ in (10 mm to 15 mm) in diameter, used for twisting wire tight.

CARPENTER'S BRACE. A brace with a selection of bits will be necessary if you need to drill any holes. If you are using $\frac{1}{2}$ in (13 mm) coach bolts you will find a 9/16th bit the best size for them.

PLUMBER'S STILSONS. A pair of these are useful for gripping and turning rusty old nuts and bolts.

ADJUSTABLE SPANNER. This can be used with almost any size of nut and saves carrying a whole boxful of spanners around with you.

WIRE BRUSH. This will remove rust and dirt from old nuts and bolts.

OIL. Penetrating oil can be sprayed on nuts and bolts or anything which is rusted up, to help free it.

SHEARS. A stout pair of ordinary garden shears can be used for trimming thorn hedges, birch, and materials incorporated in brush fences. Also useful for the same purpose is a good pair of long handled *pruners*, preferably with some sort of gear action, which will cut stems up to 2 ins (5 cm) thick.

SHOVEL. If you are going to be moving a lot of earth or stone by hand you will need a shovel as well as a spade.

FENCING MALL. For driving stakes into the ground by hand this is preferable to a sledgehammer. It has a very large, round, flat head and will not damage the top of the stake as easily as an ordinary sledgehammer. As a fencing mall is usually made of cast iron, be careful not to use it for hitting any steel spikes or pegs, which might shatter the head.

AXE. To remove roots or small trees from woodland paths on a cross-country course, an axe can be useful, but it is an unwieldy tool which requires skilful handling.

SLASHER. This long-handled implement with a blade on the end can be used for trimming hedges, cutting undergrowth, and lopping low branches off trees.

RAKE. This will be useful if you have to clear up a lot of rubbish.

TOW CHAIN. A strong chain about 10 ft (3 m) long, with links about $\frac{1}{3}$ in (10 mm) in diameter and with a ring on one end and a hook on the other, is useful for dragging timber or for towing vehicles and anything else that is heavy.

TIMBER-LIFTING TONGS. If you have to handle a lot of heavy timber manually it is worth having a pair of these, which are like hooked scissors with a handle on the end. When fitted over a log they grip it tightly, making it easier to lift, as you do not have to put your fingers underneath or bend down so far.

TURNING LEVER. This useful piece of forestry equipment consists of a bar with a hook attached to it. It can be used for rolling a log along the ground or to rotate it into position on a fence to ensure that the straightest part of it is at the top. If your top rails are big enough to make a solid and imposing-looking fence they will probably be too heavy to lift by hand.

HIGH-LIFT JACK. This will help you to lift heavy rails into position. It consists of a stout steel bar about 4 ft (1.2 m) high with a series of holes in it, and with a plate on the bottom to stop it sinking into the ground. The lifting foot is attached to a ratchet mechanism which is raised up the steel bar by using a handle. A pair of high-lift jacks will raise a top rail to the required height and will hold it in position while you measure the fence and check the height. *Important* It is possible for the pole to move slightly to one side or the other when held in the air, and for the whole lot to collapse sideways. Be careful about this. When you want to lower the jack there is a small lever which you activate. Always make sure that the handle is in the upward position when the lever is tripped; if in the downward position, the handle might fly up into the air and could hit you on the head or otherwise injure you if you are in the way.

The jack can also be used with a chain attached to it for pulling out posts. When turned into a horizontal position it can be used for straining up lengths of wire tight, or even as a small winch to pull along a heavy log or extract a vehicle which is stuck.

Timber-lifting tongs.

Turning lever.

A pair of high-lift jacks, a turning lever, and tongs.

If you do not have a high-lift jack or similar tool you will need some form of FORKED PROPS for holding the rails in position while you check the size of the fence. You might be lucky enough to find a suitably forked tree-branch which you can cut down. Or you might be able to get a blacksmith to weld a fork prop out of some steel tube — but make sure that there is a large enough plate on the bottom to stop it sinking into the ground with the weight of the rail.

If you are using several mechanical pieces of equipment it is worthwhile to have a *set of spanners* and *sockets* and *screwdrivers*. You can then carry out necessary running repairs when on the course site, thus saving time. You will need a spanner to tension the chain on your chainsaw and a file to sharpen it.

Other essential items are:

NAILS. It is advisable to have 4 in (10 cm), 5 in (12 cm), and 6 in (15 cm) nails. If you can get hold of them 8 in (20 cm) nails are very useful, as they will go right through a railway sleeper or through a large half-round rail.

WIRE. Number 8-gauge or 4 mm soft galvanised wire is recommended. This can be twisted up tight to hold timber together, though it is very stiff. You might prefer to use 10-gauge wire, which is easier to twist but is more likely to break.

Fencing-wire and rope.

STAPLES. A variety are available but $1\frac{1}{2}$ in (35 mm) ones are the most useful.

Also recommended is $\frac{3}{4}$ in (18 mm) circumference or $\frac{1}{4}$ in (6 mm) diameter polypropylene rope for tying on the top rails.

With your own selection of the above items you should be well prepared to go out and start putting together cross-country fences.

TIMBER

The size and type of timber used for building your course will not only determine whether the fences are pleasing to look at but also the way in which they are jumped and how long they will last. A fence built of big, solid timber is much more inviting to both horse and rider than one made with thin, weak-looking timber. Horses will have greater respect for fences which look too solid to knock down.

If you use sturdy timber it is not likely to get broken during the course of a competition, thus saving the course-builder anxiety and embarrassment. It will also withstand constant rubbing by live-stock, so that the effects of rot and decay will be delayed.

The ROUND POLE, usually in its rustic form with the bark left on, is the basic component of all cross-country courses.

Local sawmills and forestry contractors should be able to supply poles of the required length and diameter, though prices may vary considerably. Your own ideas of what will make a good top rail may differ considerably from that of a timber merchant, so it is always advisable to see the timber you have ordered before it is delivered; it is expensive to transport, and a contractor will not be pleased if you do not like what he brings you and ask him to take it away again. Fences built of timber with the bark left on look very smart during the first year in which they are used. After one or two years the timber will dry out and the bark will start to fall off. You must then remove it altogether; and it is surprising how it can drop off one part of the pole and stick as though glued to another, making it very difficult to shift. When the bark has come off the timber it usually leaves the fixings loose, so they will need tightening. It may also expose hidden knots on which a horse could knock himself; these must also be removed. Once all the bark has been stripped off, a coat of light golden creosote will quickly smarten up the fences again.

SPRUCE or PINE poles will last three to six years, depending on their quality. You may consider this to be a poor return for your investment, but bear in mind that you will probably want to alter the course during that time anyway.

One way to increase the life expectancy of your course is to use TREATED TIMBER, the prime example being TELEGRAPH (TELEPHONE) POLES. They have creosote forced into them under pressure, which protects the timber from the onslaught of rot and decay. They may, however, be difficult to obtain. If you are lucky enough to find along the roadside some that have taken down, ask the foreman if he can let you have them. He may want to get rid of them, and they will be relatively cheap. You will have no choice over the length and diameter of the poles, and they will arrive with an assortment of ironmongery attached to them which will have to be removed before you can use them. Alternatively, you may be able to buy some from a farmer or dealer, but one warning — the only part of treated timber which can rot is at its very centre. Poles that have been left lying in a heap on the ground for a long time may look perfect on the outside, but all of their insides may have rotted away. You can check for this by hitting them with a hammer or even kicking them with your boot to see if they sound hollow.

Another way of prolonging the life of your course is to use new timber which has been treated by the modern *tanalising* or *celcure* method. This involves peeling off the bark, drying the timber, and then putting it into a large sealed vessel. The treating chemical is then pumped into the vessel until the pressure is such that it is forced into the timber. The life of this timber should be from 30 to 50 years. Obviously, the process is expensive. It is relatively easy to get short lengths of timber such as posts treated in this manner, but longer rails are more of a problem. The bark can be removed from short lengths by a mechanical peeler, but longer lengths will not fit into most machines, so the poles have to be peeled by hand which is time-consuming and costly.

The weakest parts of a cross-country fence are the posts, which rot just where they enter the ground. It is much more important, therefore, for the posts to be 'treated' than rails which last longer because they are suspended in the air away from the moisture on the ground. Creosote painted on to timber will help it to resist very wet or dry weather, but it needs renewing annually; simply painting it on to the timber will have a negligible effect on its life compared with correct pressure treatment.

Types of Timber

Many different types of timber can be used for building courses. The following are available in Britain.

CONIFEROUS TREES provide the timber most commonly used by course builders. Of these *larch* undoubtedly is the best and the most useful. It grows relatively straight without much taper, and has few knots, while its life expectancy is considerably greater than that of most other varieties.

NORWEGIAN SPRUCE grows very straight, but tapers badly: a 24 ft (7 m) long pole could be 1 ft (30 cm) in diameter at one end and only 6 ins (15 cm) at the other. It is usually covered with small knots which are a nuisance to remove.

SCOTS PINE is prone to twisting, and has knots and rather unattractive bark.

CORSICAN PINE grows fairly straight without taper, but tends to rot quickly.

HARDWOODS, such as *oak* or *chestnut* are not usually straight enough and have too much taper to be used as rails, but they are suitable as posts. In the United States hardwoods also include *red cedar, locust, ash, hickory, ironwood* and *maple*; SOFTWOODS — which seldom last longer than two or three seasons at the most, but which are highly decorative — would include *birch, poplar, aspen* and *silver beech*.

WASTE PRODUCTS such as *slab wood scarfing* or *offcuts* can usually be obtained from a sawmill. When a log is fed through the saw mill, the first piece of timber to come off is flat on one side while the other side

Sawmill offcuts on half-rounds.

67

Railway sleepers on posts.

is slightly curved, and often still has the bark left on it. These pieces are extremely useful for filling in under fences such as palisades (see page 90), for making roofs on spread fences such as pheasant feeders, and for many other functions on the course. They are usually inexpensive.

RAILWAY SLEEPERS (RAILROAD TIES) are used on almost every cross-country course. The wood is heavily impregnated with creosote, so it lasts a long time. They are most useful for revetting ditches, making steps, reinforcing banks, and for making 'table' type obstacles. They can usually be obtained from dealers found advertising in the agricultural press, and may vary in price considerably.

Dimensions

The dimensions of the timber that you need will depend on the standard of the competition — but do bear in mind that it is always better to have it too big than too small. Smaller fences need shorter supporting posts than the higher fences. 6 ft (1.8 m) posts are about the right length to use for Novice and Pony Club fences of height 3 ft 6 in (1.07 m), while 7 ft (2.1 m) posts are recommended for fences up to 4 ft (1.2 m) high. When 8 ft (2.4 m) poles are used as the standard length, fences may be 16 ft (4.9 m), 24 ft (7.3 m), or 32 ft (9.8 m) wide, depending on the type or height of obstacle, with a post at every join. Strong, treated or untreated timber may be very heavy, but these lengths can usually be lifted up by one man. They have the added advantage that if hit hard by a horse only one section of a fence will be damaged and can be repaired quickly. Also, uniform timber without taper is more readily available in 8 ft (2.4 m) sections. These lengths are particularly suitable for building fences on undulating ground, so that the height of every part can be set accurately. However, you can where necessary cut a pole to the exact length required. Posts should have a minimum diameter of 6 to

Example of a wide, solid-looking fence.

7 in (15 to 18 cm) for Novice or Pony Club fences, rising to 8 to 10 in (20 to 25 cm) for larger and Advanced fences. At least one third of a post's length should be in the ground. Remember that if the ground dips or slopes away where the posts are positioned, or if the posts are situated in a ditch, they will need to be considerably longer.

Generally speaking, the wider a fence the more inviting it is to jump. A typically narrow obstacle, such as a stile, should not be less than 6 ft (1.8 m) wide and will certainly need wings. A fence set in a natural fencing line can be narrower than an island fence, but should be no less than 18 ft (5.5 m) wide. Even then it would look more inviting with Christmas trees or some type of wing on either side.

Wings on fences always make the obstacle easier to jump and may also make it more attractive. They tend to 'frame' a fence, thus drawing the eye towards it. The wings themselves must be made of material which complements that used in the obstacle. They should always be higher than the obstacle, otherwise horses and riders will find it difficult to centre on where they are supposed to jump. Straw bales, hurdles, posts and rails, and shrubs, all form suitable wing material. The tendency to use Christmas trees by every fence can be overdone, and they often look unnatural. The types of obstacle which really must have wings are those sited in the middle of a field — i.e. island fences — and those set in a wire boundary fence. As

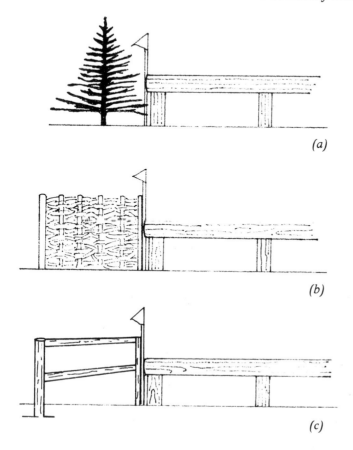

(a)

(b)

(c)

Types of wing
(a) *Fir tree.*
(b) *Hurdle.*
(c) *Angled rails.*

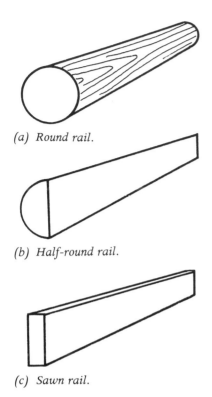

(a) Round rail.

(b) Half-round rail.

(c) Sawn rail.

many obstacles as possible should be sited close to trees, bushes, shrubs, etc., which will form natural wings.

It is useful to have your top rail lengths in multiples of your post lengths, for example an 18 ft (5.5 m) top rail can be cut into three 6 ft (1.8 m) posts, a 21 ft (6.4 m) rail can be cut into three 7 ft (2.1 m) posts. Top rails should be a minimum of 7 to 8 in (18 to 20 cm) diameter for Novice (Preliminary) and smaller fences, and up to between 8 and 10 in (20 to 25 cm) for larger fences. *If you can pick up your top rails easily by hand, they are probably not big enough.* Round poles can be split down the middle to make half-rounds. A big, strong half-round may be used as the top rail of a straightforward type of fence, with the advantage that it can simply be nailed on to the posts. However, half-round rails are more often used as the lower rails of a fence which need not be as large or as heavy as the top rail. The easiest way to split poles is at a sawmill on a circular or band saw, although the lengths they can cut are sometimes limited. It is possible to cut poles down the middle using a chainsaw, which has the advantage that you can follow any curve that may be in the tree. To make a neat job of splitting a pole by this method requires practice.

You can also use SAWN TIMBER to build fences. When a log is sawn lengthways, the saw cut often goes at an angle across the grain of the timber, thus losing much of its natural strength; or a knot could appear in the middle of a length of timber, creating a weak spot. A sawn rail is therefore never as strong as its more natural round counterpart, so if you use sawn rails they should be no less than 5 in × 3 in (12 cm × 8 cm) and will need supporting at least every 6 ft (1.8 m) along their length.

Finally, a supply of HALF-ROUND FARM FENCING STAKES, $5\frac{1}{2}$ ft to 6 ft (1.7 m to 1.8 m) long, and approximately 4 in (10 cm) in diameter, may be needed, especially for holding up your sleepers when revetting ditches and building banks and steps. These should be pressure treated if you want them to last longer than ten years.

3 TYPES OF OBSTACLE

(a) Posts and Rails

The post and rail fence is fundamental to all cross-country courses. It can be constructed in several different ways, the most satisfactory being to rope ROUND RAILS to ROUND POSTS and to support them on DUMMY POSTS.

It is also possible to bolt round rails to round posts, or to fit round rails into V-shaped notches on the top of round posts.

Sawn rails can be roped, nailed, bolted, or notched to various types of posts.

The two main advantages of the first method are (1) that the fence is extremely strong because the pressure of a horse hitting the rail is taken directly against the side of the main post, and (2) that the ropes which secure the rail can be cut quickly if it is necessary to extricate a horse which is trapped.

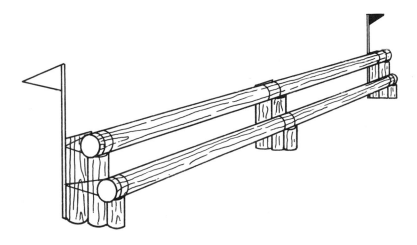

Post and rails: round posts roped to round rails, on dummy posts.

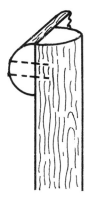

Half-round rail nailed to half-round post.

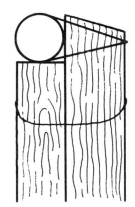

Round rail roped to round post, on dummy post.

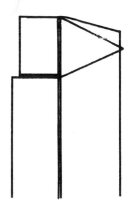

Sawn rail roped to post, with dummy post.

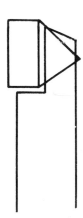

Sawn rail notched and roped to post.

Stages of building a fence
Post driven in alongside pre-positioned rail.

Below: *Top rail offered up on jacks or props for measurement and observation.*

Above, left: *Digging small hole for dummy post.*

Above, right: *Attaching dummy post with twisted wire.*

Cutting off post top with chainsaw.

Lower rail on dummy post (side view detail).

Construction completed.

A DUMMY POST is versatile. It can be cut off to lower a rail or made higher by inserting a block. The lower rail fitted on the dummy post comes out in front of the line of the top rail, giving the fence a slightly ascending shape, which makes it more inviting to jump than a straight vertical.

Method of Construction

☐ To build a post and rail fence using the above method, first select the top rail and lie it directly beneath its eventual intended position. Before you put the posts into the ground you can then check that the exact siting of the fence is correct in relation to the lie of the surrounding land. If your rail is between 9 ft and 18 ft (3 m and 5.5 m) long you will need three posts. A rail between 18 ft and 27 ft (5.5 m and 8.2 m) long needs four posts. In the USA the lengths are generally in 8 ft (2.4 m) sections, so shorter rails and more posts are used, and the standard fence is 24 ft (7 m) wide.

☐ If you are using a mechanical (tractor-mounted) post-driver to sink the posts in the ground, simply drive in the posts up against the rail where it lies. This will ensure that they are in a straight line and the right distance apart. Although the efficiency of the particular machine and the type of ground must be considered, you may find it better not to point the posts. If the point hits any form of obstruction underground — such as a stone or a root — it will be driven off course and the post will then slant one way or the other. A blunt post may take slightly longer to drive in, but it will push down any obstruction underneath it and will be more likely to go in straight.

☐ Round posts are usually smaller at one end than the other, and you should drive the smaller end into the ground so that the post acts like a wedge and goes in tight. Even for simple schooling fences they should be at least 5 in (13 cm) in diameter.

☐ When using a post-driving machine, make a habit of keeping your hand away from the top of the post at all times.

☐ If you are putting the rail up against a hedge or on the edge of a ditch it may not be possible to sink the posts with the rail in position. Instead, before moving the rail out of the way, you will have to mark where each post is to go by digging out a turf. Whether you bore the holes with a mechanical post-hole borer or dig them by hand you will have to move away the rail, to give yourself room to work and to make room to put the loose earth or spoil.

☐ To be strong, a post should have at least one-third of its length in the ground. When you have made your hole deep enough, put the post in and stand it upright. Shovel some earth back in the hole a little at a time and thump it down very firmly, using the end of a stake or a purpose-designed thumper. Do not use the end of a wooden-handled shovel or rake; the handle will be ruined. *Make sure that the posts are tightly secured in the ground*; when they are, you can then offer up your top rail.

☐ Even if the rail is light enough to lift up by hand you will almost certainly need to find a way of holding it in position, as you must measure the fence and stand back to assess if it is the right height. The easiest way to do this is to use a pair of high-lift jacks to support each end of the rail. The jacks can lift up the rail from the ground, and the height of each end can be adjusted a little at a time. Alternatively, you can use forked props which can be adjusted by moving the base further in or out as required. Another method is to lift up the rail and hold it in position, using the arms on the front of a tractor. The disadvantage of this method is that the tractor is in the way, which makes it difficult to stand back and look at the fence.

☐ Use a spirit level which is long enough to reach from the top of the rail back to above where a horse would take off. You can then read the height of the fence. Every part of it which could be jumped should measure within the height limit allowed for the competition. When you have adjusted the pole to comply with the rules, stand back and look at it; in certain situations, it could still be too difficult for the competition.

☐ Once you have decided that the rail is in the correct place, secure it temporarily to one of the posts with a piece of rope; this will prevent it from falling on you or from coming down while you are completing the fixing procedure. To support the weight of the top rail the *dummy post* should be at least half the diameter of the rail. Dig out a small square of turf about 4 in (10 cm) deep immediately in front of each of the main posts and underneath the rail. Measure from the bottom of this hole to the underside of the top rail, then cut yourself a piece of timber to that length. Place the dummy post in the small hole and underneath the rail. You may have to raise the rail slightly, but make sure that it returns to the correct position. When it is exactly in the right place the dummy post can be wired to the main post by twisting a piece of wire around the two pieces of timber and stapling it down firmly.

When all the dummy posts have been fitted in position you will be ready to rope the top rail to the main posts. To do this, use polypropylene rope $\frac{1}{4}$ in (6 mm) in diameter. (1) Knot the rope. (2) Increase the tension by winding the spare end round to give you a mechanical advantage, like a pulley. (3) Pull the end to draw the two parallel pieces of rope together, increasing the tension. (4) When the two pieces of rope have met, wind the end round several more turns to make a neat and tidy job. (See diagrams.)

Having roped the rail to all the posts, trim off the tops at a downward angle, away from the rail, being careful not to cut the ropes at the same time. To achieve a tidy finish, rasp or surform the cut edges of the posts to remove any whiskers and the sharp edges. You may also square off both ends of the rail where they project beyond the posts, but always leave 2 in or 3 in (5 cm or 8 cm) of overhang.

☐ If a half-round lower rail is being used, offer it up either on the jacks or props or by suspending it from the top rail, using ropes. Stand back and look at it to make sure that it is in a level position at roughly half the height of the top rail.

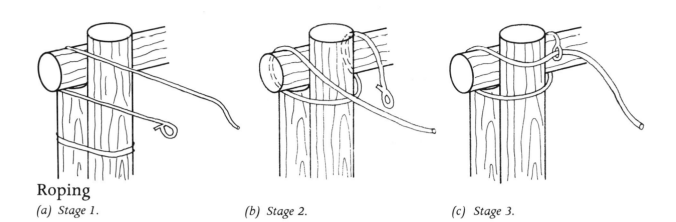

Roping

(a) Stage 1.

(b) Stage 2.

(c) Stage 3.

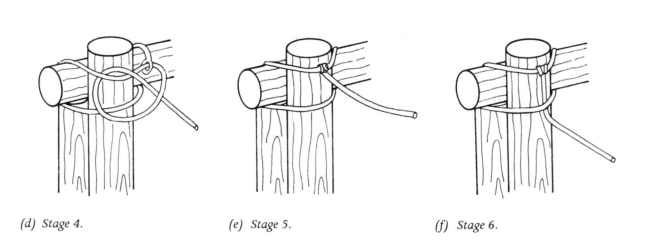

(d) Stage 4.

(e) Stage 5.

(f) Stage 6.

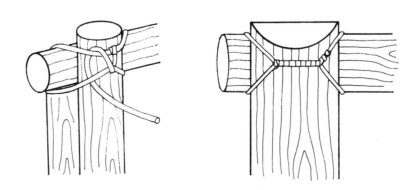

(g) Stage 7.

(h) Stage 8.

Round top rail on dummy post, roped. Half-round lower rail on chocks.

When the lower rail is in position, nail it securely at one end only, either using 6 in or 8 in (15 cm or 20 cm) nails. Then cut out a V-shaped chock from a spare piece of half-round timber and nail it under the other end of the rail. This is enough to support it, yet the rail can be released if a horse should put his legs between the top and lower rails. If chocks are used at both ends the rail can fall off too easily when a horse hits the fence hard. It could also be knocked off by livestock, and after lying on the ground it will leave its mark just in front of the fence.

If you use a round lower rail it will have to be supported on a smaller set of dummy posts wired to the front of the existing, taller, dummies. It should be secured by rope and therefore will not fly out if a horse gets trapped in it: it will be released only by cutting the ropes. The dummy posts should be levelled off, so that the rail will slide off easily if the ropes are cut.

To make this type of fence more upright, the dummy post can be cut in two, so that the lower rail can fit between the two parts and up against the main post. Cut off the ends of the lower rail, square with the ends of the top rail, and surform them.

□ To build a fence by fitting round rails on top of the main posts themselves, offer up the top rail as before, then mark the side of the posts level with the underside of the rail. Next, lower the rail out of the way and cut a V-shaped notch at the top of the post. When you have cut all the posts, lift the rail into position. You may have to adjust some of your notches until the rail sits comfortably in all of

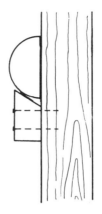

Half-round lower rail, resting in V-shaped chock.

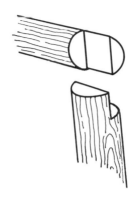

Round rail attached to round post, halved.

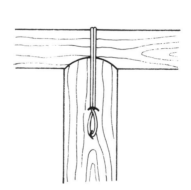

Rail wired or roped, and stapled to notched post.

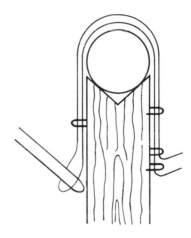

Stapling a rail on to a notched post.

them. Then fix the rail, either by putting a loop of wire over the top of it and stapling it to both sides of the post, or by drilling through the rail downwards and driving a bolt, or steel pin, into the top of the post. The disadvantages of this method of construction are that if a horse becomes trapped in the fence the rail cannot be lowered easily, and it is very difficult to adjust the height after the fence has been completed. It is also possible that the back of the post could split away and the rail could fall to the ground if it is hit very hard. Lower rails can be fitted to the front of the posts in the same way as in the previous method of construction.

☐ You can also fit round rails to round posts by notching, or halving the post and/or the rail. You can then rope the rails on, but the disadvantage of this method is that it weakens both the post and the rail, and if the timber is to be used again for another job the notches are likely to be in the wrong place and will look unsightly.

LIGHTWEIGHT RAILS may be *bolted to the posts* with ½-in (13 mm)

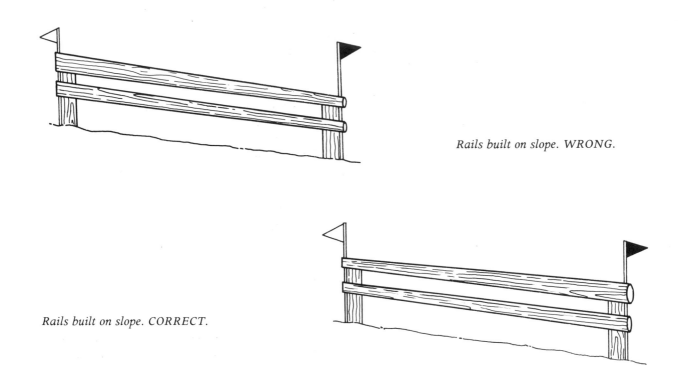

Rails built on slope. WRONG.

Rails built on slope. CORRECT.

Sawn rails, nailed and roped.

80

coach bolts. Drilling holes with a brace and bit through new green timber is a laborious business; and again, dismantling the fence can be a lengthy operation.

HALF-ROUND RAILS which are substantial enough (minimum 5 in × 3 in or 13 cm × 8 cm thick) to be used *as the top rail of a fence* can simply be nailed on to posts, making sure that the nails are large enough. This method is useful when making the permanent framework of fences such as pheasant feeders or seats. (See page 100.) It is obviously quicker and cheaper than using dummy posts, round rails, rope and wire.

SAWN RAILS can either be nailed or bolted directly on to their posts, or a small notch can be cut out of the front of the post just large enough to carry the weight of the rail. The rail can then be roped on as before.

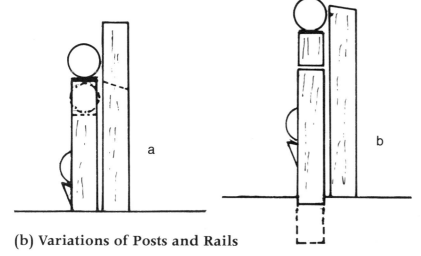

Raising and lowering a rail
(a) To lower, cut off dummy post to required height. Level off back post. (b) To raise, insert block above or under the dummy to achieve required height. Back post must cover at least 50 per cent of rail when raised. Remember to raise lower rail, approximately half-way between top rail and ground.

(b) Variations of Posts and Rails

A SINGLE POST AND RAIL is not a very inspiring obstacle and should not appear too often on a course. When added to or varied, however, it can be adapted as an important basis of many different fences.

TWO POSTS AND RAILS, one immediately behind the other, make a PARALLEL. The back rail of a parallel should always be slightly higher than the front rail, so that it is clearly visible to both horse and rider. It is important that the rails of a parallel should be roped on, as this is the type of fence in which a horse can be caught up. A lower rail on the rear section serves no useful purpose and could be dangerous.

THREE POSTS AND RAILS one behind the other constitute a TRIPLE BAR. This is generally built with the first rail quite close to the ground, the third one at nearly maximum height, and the one in the middle half way between the height of the other two, giving it an ascending shape. It can also be constructed by lying the middle and lower rail on a sloping strut which is attached at one end to the side or front of the main post. The other (front) end rests on — or is dug into — the ground. If a triple bar is built with a very wide base spread it tends to

Triple Bar.

Parallel (oxer).

look low and flat, and as it could cause a horse to paddle in between the rails, it should be avoided.

To build a fence of maximum base spread and maximum height, a fourth rail can be introduced. The back rail is at maximum height, the next rail nearest to it only slightly lower, and the lower two rails are as for a triple bar, giving the fence a rounded profile which is more attractive and safer.

HELSINKI STEPS. Posts and rails built on the side of a slope. If the slope is not too steep, a step-like effect can be gained between each section of rails by setting the higher pole on top of the lower one. If the slope is steeper, the different levels can be achieved by putting a block between the two rails. When offering up the rails of a Helsinki Steps

fence, do not use a spirit level to set the angle of the top rail — as when horizontal they will appear to rise sharply in the air at the 'downhill' end. Site them by judging with your eye until each rail appears to be horizontal: there will be less difference in height between each end of the sections, and this will minimise the amount of the fence that may exceed the maximum height allowed.

Helsinki Steps.

Helsinki Steps:
Left: *Detail, with block.*
Right: *Detail, without block.*

Ditch 'towards'.

DITCH 'TOWARDS' and DITCH 'AWAY'. Posts and rails built either on the take-off or landing side of a ditch.

TRAKEHNER. Posts and rails over the centre of a ditch, or angled from one side of a ditch to another. A fence built immediately over the centre of a ditch will need extra long posts, particularly if the bottom of the ditch is soft. A fence angled from one bank of the ditch to the other can only have a post at either end of the rail. Therefore both the rail and the posts must be extremely strong and the posts must be very secure in the ground.

It may be necessary for the posts of a Trakehner (or any other fence where the posts are subject to undue stress) to have additional support in the form of a *Godfather*. This is a strut sloping down from a notch cut into the top part of the post to the ground in the direction in which it is likely to be moved. The end is dug into the ground and a large stone or block is placed against it to stop it pushing further into the ground. The same method is used for supporting the strainer posts of wire fences. Alternatively, the rail over a ditch may rest on a horizontal bar at either end, attached to posts on either side of the ditch, with chocks nailed on to secure it in position. The advantage of this method is that the rail can easily be adjusted to alter the nature and difficulty of the obstacle.

Trakehner on posts.

Trakehner over water. Pole resting on notched posts and secured with rope. Note the 'Godfather' or strut which suggests that the fence is designed to be jumped in the other direction (left to right).

Elephant Trap. Rails resting on blocks. Top rail may also be roped. Note the supporting strut.

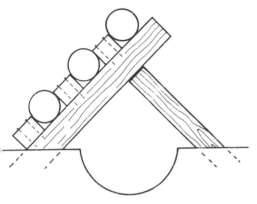

ELEPHANT TRAP. Another way of presenting a rail over the middle of a ditch. This fence is built on sloping posts which must be very securely fixed, with at least half their length in the ground, and with the soil firmly rammed back around them; otherwise, if a horse comes down heavily on to the rail the impact can lever the ends of the post out of the ground. The risk of this happening can be avoided by fixing a similar post on the opposite side of the ditch, to add extra support. The rails should be roped to the posts and rest on chocks, so that they can be moved or lowered easily if a horse should become hung up. (For this reason, a knife-rest joint, formed where the two posts cross over at the top, cannot be recommended although it is easier to build. The rail would be trapped and could only be released by using a saw.)

TIGER TRAP. This is similar to an Elephant Trap, but has a lower rail resting on the additional far-sided posts. For a competition in which the fence will always be jumped in one direction only, the lower rails on the landing side are unnecessary, and they can also be dangerous.

Tiger Trap.

Log pile. A useful obstacle as it can be designed to be jumped from either direction.

Tyres firmly secured in a wooden frame. As they are identical from either side they can also be jumped in the other direction.

Zig-zag rails over a natural ditch.

'Echelon' or staggered rails.

Fan.

Log fence. When short lengths of
wood are used to make this type of
log pile they must be fixed extra
securely, so that if a horse hits the
top nearside edge, or banks the
obstacle, the timber will not move.
A framework achieves this, as seen
here, but beware of making a false
groundline. If level on top, this fence
can be jumped in either direction.

Coop or pheasant feeder. A useful
obstacle as it can also be jumped
from the other side.

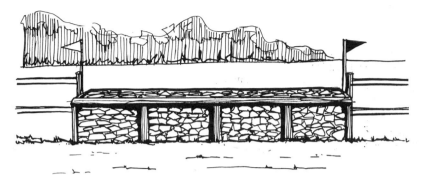

Artificial wall. If the top is level it can be jumped in both directions.

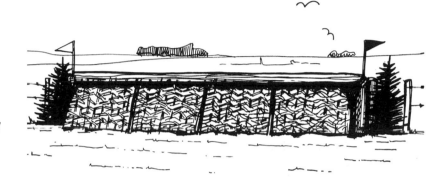

Hurdles, used as a filling in a solid fence.

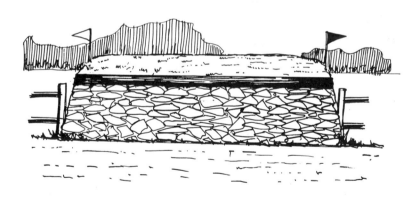

Stone-faced bank turfed on the top. Can be jumped from either direction.

Stile, another 'reversible' design.

Detail of the top of a palisade built on a post and rail framework. The vertical scarfing on both sides makes this obstacle jumpable in either direction.

Panel of horizontal half-round rails.

(c) Fences with a Post and Rail Framework

PALISADE. This usually has a round or strong half-round top rail, with upright boards, slats, or sawmill offcuts nailed on to the top rail and dug into the ground — either vertically below the top rail or slightly out in front — to give it a sloping appearance. It can be built entirely of half-round rails nailed horizontally to make a solid wall.

These two types of obstacle are useful when built over a wire livestock fence. Sandwich the wire between the posts and the rail so that there is no dangerous gap between the wire and the timber, into which a horse could drop a leg. You may need to remove or lower the top strand of wire and to put high guard rails or wings about 12 ft (3.5 m) wide on either side of the obstacle, as protection against a horse running out at the fence.

BALUSTRADE. This has a series of vertical round or half-round timbers underneath the top rail, with gaps between each one. The gaps must be wide enough (less than 3 ins, 8 cm; or more than 8 ins, 20 cm) to prevent a horse's foot from getting trapped. Round posts can have a V-shaped notch cut in the top so they fit directly under a round top rail. If a half-round top rail is used, the posts can be notched and nailed on to the back — though this may give the fence a slightly false groundline which would then need an additional lower rail half-way down across the front.

STILE. This should always be built in a natural fence line. If a post and rail stile already exists you may be able to retain it, at least for the lower part of the fence, but you will need to add some stronger

90

posts and to reinforce the top rail, while making the obstacle look as natural as possible. A step added underneath should be angled and should have no sharp edges.

Balustrade.

SHARK'S TEETH. This is a post and rail with angled struts nailed to the top rail and dug into the ground in front of the obstacle. It is important that where the struts meet on the top rail they should be far enough apart for a horse's foot to pass easily between them. If they form a completely closed 'V' they could act like a boot-jack and trap a horse's foot.

Shark's teeth and parallel.

Hayrack.

HAYRACK. Basically a parallel rail filled in with sloping slats. If the slats are of light material, widely spaced, and going deep into the gap between the rails, the middle should be reinforced with some additional form of timber strong enough to withstand a horse's weight. Alternatively, the slats should be strong, close enough together, and reasonably shallow, so that a horse could tread on them without getting into trouble.

SEAT. This has a framework of posts and rails, with a low rail built out in front to form the leading edge of the seat itself. Slats can then be nailed on to form the seat and the backrest. The horizontal slats should be strong enough and close enough together to support the weight of a horse treading on them. You will have to use your 'eye' to make the proportions of the seat correct. Make sure that the base is not too wide, causing the fence to look too 'flat' for its height.

Seat.

Seat. Detail of side.

(d) Posts and Rails for Alternative and Combination Fences

When building these more complicated fences you may need to join rails together either in a straight line or at angles, and to form corners. Joining rails on the outside of the bend or angle is relatively straightforward. Try and find two rails of the same diameter, as this will obviously make a neater-looking joint. Cut the rails at an angle so that they fit compactly against each other, and rope them as if they were one continuous piece of wood.

Joining rails on a straight line or on the inside of a bend or angle is not quite so easy. If they are simply butted together it is possible that because of the roundness of the post a horse hitting the rail hard will

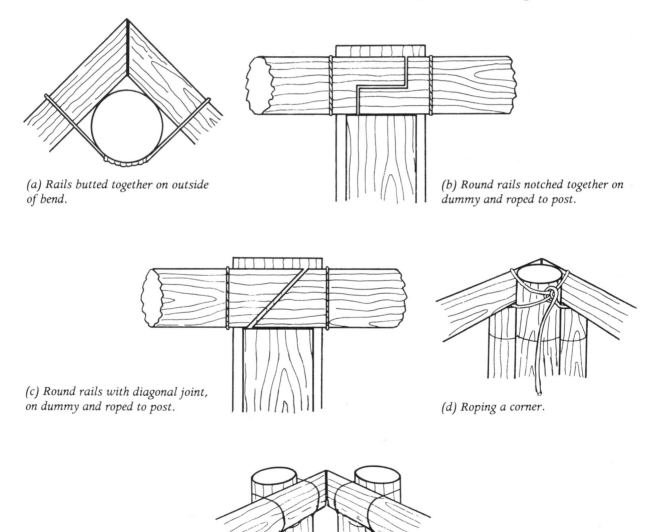

(a) Rails butted together on outside of bend.

(b) Round rails notched together on dummy and roped to post.

(c) Round rails with diagonal joint, on dummy and roped to post.

(d) Roping a corner.

(e) Inverted corner: rails butted together on dummy posts.

Rails notched at corner post.

knock it past the post. As this obviously must be avoided, again choose rails of similar diameter, and cut out the bottom half from one — about the thickness of the post along the rail — and the top half from the other, the same distance along its length. Then sit one on top of the other, and again rope them as one. This will give both rails a very good bearing on the post, even if they are round the inside of a bend. Alternatively, if you want to avoid too much carpentry, use two posts relatively close together, on either side of the join.

When building a CORNER FENCE put the rails on either side of the post at the corner. Place half of the rope over one rail and the other half over the other. Make sure that the next post along on the back rail of the corner is a really strong one, and that it is not too far from the corner. 6½ ft or 2 m should be satisfactory. If a horse makes a mistake when jumping, this is where he will hit the fence very hard and it must therefore be the strongest part of the whole construction.

Tree trunk raised above ground and secured with posts and roping.

LARGE LOGS or TREE TRUNKS can be used in much the same way as a post and rail. The posts should be knocked in the ground, to prevent the logs being moved by a horse, and blocks should be wedged under them to hold them at the right height. Do not rely on a log staying in position under its own weight. A horse hitting it with his chest could move it.

(e) Other Types of Fence
Many other materials can be used for making cross-country obstacles.

RAILWAY SLEEPERS (RAILROAD TIES). These are very useful for making several types of fence. A plain SLEEPER WALL should be at least two sleepers wide to be inviting. The sleepers can be simply nailed, wired, or roped, to stout upright posts. To make them more interesting, arrange the sleepers in the shape of a 'V' or zig-zag.

SLOPING SLEEPER FENCE. This makes a useful downhill obstacle. Attach angled struts to the front of your vertical posts, lay the sleepers on them, and nail them down securely. The advantages of this type of fence are that if a horse refuses and slides into it, the sleepers will withstand a horse's weight; and if the horse scrambles over it — because it is alarmed by the drop — or if it drops its hind legs, again the sleepers will give solid support and the horse will be unlikely to hurt himself.

SLEEPER TABLE and CHURN-STAND. These make solid, permanent fences. To build one, put the posts in the ground at the corners of the fence and in the middle where the sleepers will join. To carry the sleepers you will need some stout horizontal bearers to go between the posts. It is often easiest to use a sleeper or part-sleeper itself as the bearer. Work out the required height, then cut off the posts at that height, minus the thickness of a sleeper and the thickness of a bearer added together. It is always best to leave the posts a little too high and to offer up the sleepers and bearers on the top, then to take a little more off — rather than to cut a post too short, as it will be difficult to pack it out to make it higher. When you are sure that you have the posts cut off level and at the correct height, nail or wire the bearers down on the top, then fix the sleepers on to the bearers. Either use wire, which tends to look untidy, or 8 in (20 cm) nails. Otherwise, drill $\frac{7}{16}$ in (approx 11 mm) holes through the sleepers and partially into the bearer then drive in a $\frac{1}{2}$ in (13 mm) bolt or length of rod which will fit tightly in the $\frac{7}{16}$ in (11 mm) hole, and hold the sleepers down very firmly — though it may be a problem to lift them up again if you want to dismantle the fence.

Sleepers can be used as lower rails for the table or as a complete wall down the front. This is also a convenient way of building an obstacle over a wire livestock fence.

Sleeper wall built over a wire fence.

Sleeper wall, sloping, seen from take-off side.

Sleeper wall, sloping, seen from landing side.

Sleeper table/churn stand. Note that wings will be necessary to cover the wire fence.

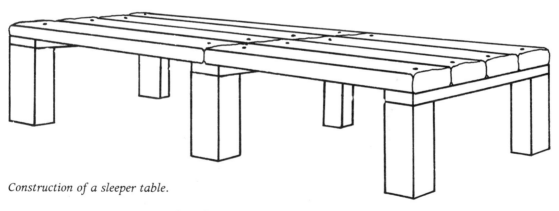

Construction of a sleeper table.

TABLE. This can be made out of any sawn timber, as long as it is strong enough to support a horse's weight should it be banked. Round poles can also be used, but make sure that they fit tightly together so that there are no gaps into which a horse could drop a leg.

TROUGH. This is simply a table with sides which form a rim all the way round the edge. It is advisable to have the posts on the outside of a trough so that they give support to the sides as well as the underneath, but make sure that the posts are cut off at an angle and that the edges of the sawn timber are well rasped to avoid injuring a horse. Obviously the bottom or base of the trough should be solid enough for the horse to be able to bank it safely, as in a table-type obstacle.

PHEASANT FEEDER. Another spread fence with a solid top. It can be built either with a single sloping or an apex-type roof. It will look quite natural if the top is covered with sawmill offcuts or scarfing, but there must be enough support underneath to bear a horse's weight should he bank the fence.

Half-round rails nailed on to stout round posts usually make a good framework for a pheasant feeder. When you nail the slats on to the top, and particularly if making an apex-type roof, remember that it will add to the height of the fence. This should be taken into account when fixing the top rail. The slats should not overhang the rail of the leading edge on the take-off side, so if you are going to trim off the ends after nailing the slats into position, be sure to put the nails far enough back so that you do not catch them with the saw.

WOODEN GATES. These make good natural fences. However, a standard agricultural gate is never strong enough to withstand

Gates reinforced with posts.

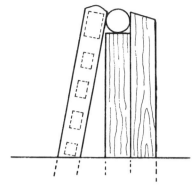

Reinforced gate.

Ornamental fence.

continuous jumping by horses. The top rail, especially, will need some reinforcement, which can best be achieved by leaning the gate against a post and rail fence, with either a solid round or half-pole behind the top bar to give the gate the required support. This obviously detracts from the natural appearance of the fence; to support the gate *without* spoiling the look of it, fix a piece of 2 in × $\frac{1}{4}$ in (50 mm × 6 mm) steel along the back of the top bar, using coach bolts. A gate is always more inviting to jump when leaning away slightly.

Try not to site an upright gate where horses can either gallop very fast at it or approach it downhill.

ORNAMENTAL FENCES. Flower beds or garden frames, for example, add variety to a course and can be attractive. The method of construction can often be inspired by, or adapted to, the local surroundings.

ROOF OR RAILED ARCH. This can be built over a fence, so that competitors will have to jump under it, but the overhead part must

Ornamental fence.

Overhead roof.

102

be well out of reach, as an inexperienced horse may 'duck' and hit the fence, or fall. The British Horse Society rules specify a minimum height of 11 ft (3.3 m) for such an obstacle. You should consider having it higher than this, especially for a Novice competition.

TIMBER WAGON. This is not difficult to build and is particularly useful if towable, as it can be sited in a variety of different places. You may be able to adapt an old farm cart, or find two pairs of wheels and axles from a scrap yard from which to build the wagon. Make sure that you leave no sharp metal edges on which a horse could hurt himself. If the construction is relatively light, you may need stakes or pegs to secure it firmly in place.

BARRELS. These can often be incorporated into fences. They are probably more use as in-fills underneath the top rail of a fence, as they are seldom high enough to make a fence on their own. They must be anchored securely so that they cannot move if a horse hits them. Do not use old metal barrels, which might break or disintegrate if trodden on, leaving dangerous, rusty, sharp edges.

STRAW BALES. These make useful 'fillers'. They should always be secured firmly so that they cannot be moved, and they will be treated with greater respect by horses if there is at least one solid pole above the bales. Bales are often used to provide a bulky framework for a birch or spruce fence.

HURDLES. Not recommended for solid obstacles, as they will break easily. They can, however, be useful fillers or wings.

SACKS. These can add variety to a course, although they tend to look garish and unnatural. If you do use them they must look solid and must be fixed securely.

TYRES. These should be of uniform size and held firm by two rails threaded through them. The rails should be forced apart and fixed securely to posts.

(f) Walls

These are ready-made obstacles in the countryside, but they will almost certainly require some form of reinforcement and protection. A half-round rail fitted along the leading edge will usually prevent the wall from being damaged and will protect horses from injury. Make sure that the rail does not project, giving the fence a false groundline; if it does, you need to insert a lower rail. The rails must be flush against the wall and not separated from it by the thickness of the stakes which hold them up, as this will leave a narrow, dangerous gap.

If your wall is strong enough not to need reinforcement, or if you are building it from scratch, you can probably fix the top rail to the wall by bedding it into mortar, or by fixing it to *bolts* or *studs* previously embedded in the mortar on the top.

A dry stone wall, even if purpose-built for the cross-country

Stone wall with embedded reinforced top rail.

course, will certainly need substantial timber reinforcements. A convenient way of making it safe and jumpable from both sides is to fix a sleeper on the top, possibly bedded into some mortar, but with stakes down both sides of the wall to anchor it firmly.

(g) Brush Fences

Natural brush fences, such as thorn hedges, grow in most parts of the country and should be incorporated in a cross-country course whenever possible. But do not think that you will be able to use every hedge on your site. Beware of the very tall, thick hedge which when cut down to the appropriate size for your course is left as a cluster of thick stumps the size of a man's arm, with sharp, jagged tops totally unsuitable for jumping. Hedges which have grown very tall can be laid, to make them a suitable size; this is a long-established technique used for keeping hedges stockproof. Individual saplings are trimmed and then partially cut through, folded over on top of each other, and woven together with stakes and binders to form a continuous and secure barrier. It is advisable to employ a local

Cut and laid hedge reinforced with rail (front view).

Cut and laid hedge reinforced with rail (rear view).

Left: *Filling a bullfinch or brush frame.*

Left below: *Filling a frame, alternative method.*

Right: *Framework for a brush fence.*

Stuffing the frame of a brush fence.

expert to lay a hedge, as to do it well and tidily is a skilled job.

Whether you are using a CUT AND LAID HEDGE, a STAKE AND BOUND HEDGE, or a BUSHY HEDGE which is neatly trimmed to the right height for your course, it will need some form of reinforcement to preserve its shape. If a large number of horses jump a hedge in its natural state, many will brush through it, and inevitably holes will be made which will become larger and will lower the fence. During a competition these holes are very difficult to repair, and it is not possible to keep the fence in the same condition all day. Timber must therefore be used to strengthen the top line of the hedge. Rules for Horse Trials in Britain state that any part of a fence which a horse can brush through without difficulty may exceed the maximum height allowed for the fence by 6 in (15 cm); USCTA rules specify 8 in (20 cm). So reinforcement rails can be up to maximum height. They should always be sited on the take-off side of the hedge and must be clearly visible to the horse. If a solid piece of timber is hidden in what appears to be a brush-through fence, the horse may easily hit the solid part of the obstacle, and might fall. Try to get the timber close into the hedge so that there is no gap between the rail and the brush.

☐ Trim the hedge so that it shows above and beyond the rail and also bushes out below the front of the rail. This is easily achieved with a mechanical post-driver, as the fence posts can be pushed right into the hedge by the tractor and then driven into the ground. Boring or digging the holes will be more difficult, because the hedge will be in the way, and if you trim it out you will spoil the look of the fence — for the first year at least. It may be possible to overcome this problem by slightly angling the posts back into the hedge.

☐ If you use the dummy post and rope method of fixing the rail you will, of course, find it impossible to tie the ropes, as you will be working inside the hedge itself. To solve this problem, treat the rail as the post and the post as the rail, so that you tie the knot vertically on the front of the rail instead of horizontally on the back of the post. Remember to leave enough of the post projecting, to prevent the rope from slipping off the top.

☐ If you have a rather meagre piece of hedge which you wish to use, you can build a *Double Oxer*. This is basically a parallel with a hedge in between the two rails. The back rail must be clearly visible above the hedge in the middle. Also, make sure that either the hedge bushes out underneath and below the front rail, or that you have a lower rail on the front section, to give the fence a good groundline.

(h) Birch Fences

If there are no natural hedges it is possible to build brush fences artificially. The most familiar is the birch fence. Birch is the material used for making steeplechase fences on racecourses and is provided by the saplings which grow up from the stumps of silver birch trees when they have been cut down. If it is cut in winter it is without leaf whereas in spring or summer it still has its leaves, making it much softer and easier for horses to brush through — though it does tend to become 'gappy' as the leaves drop off.

☐ Birch without leaves makes firm, substantial brush fences. It can usually be obtained from large forestry areas, but is expensive to buy and to transport, and you will always need more than you think. It is usually delivered in bundles about 12 in to 15 in (30 cm to 38 cm) in diameter, tied in two or three places with string. These have to be packed tightly into some form of frame.

☐ The simplest frame is made by nailing half-round rails on to both sides of standard round posts. The posts should be no more than 8 ft (2.4 m) apart and you will need one pair of rails at the top and another pair lower down. The top rail at the back — which will be on the landing side of the fence — should be set slightly lower than the top rail on the take-off side. This is a precaution, in case a horse brushes through the birch low down and catches the hidden rail. If there is an intermediate post in the frame there will be a gap immediately above the post after the birch has been tightly packed. When jumping a brush fence, horses and riders tend to aim for a weak spot, or gap. In order to reduce the size of this gap, cut the top of the intermediate post into a wedge so that the sharp edge of the wedge is at right angles to the line of the fence. This will effectively reduce the width of the post at the top and also the width of the gaps between the birch on either side of the post.

If your posts are sufficiently thick in diameter, you will be able to put whole bundles into the frame between the the two half-round rails. Start from one end and stand about three bundles in the frame. Make sure that all the butt ends of the birch saplings are level and touching the ground at the bottom. Then pass a rope round the far side of the bundles and attach it to a vehicle or tractor parked in line with the fence. Next, while one member of the team gingerly drives forward to compress the birch with the rope, the other should stand by with a crowbar or sledgehammer to tap the birch, keeping it vertical and evenly compressed. Only experience will tell you how high up to put the rope in order to get the birch to pull up evenly. It is important to keep the birch vertical, otherwise you will be in trouble when you reach the end of the frame. Tie a second piece of rope round the three bundles and secure it around the end post of the frame to anchor the bundles while the tension of the other rope is released by the vehicle. Then stack another three bundles into the frame. Put the rope round them and pull them up tight again with the tractor. Continue this process until the whole frame is evenly stuffed. You will probably have to open up the last couple of bundles at the end of each section of frame and stick the saplings in, one at a time, as the gap will not be big enough to fit in a whole bundle. When you have packed the entire frame tightly, cut all the strings and pull them out.

You will now have a 7 ft or 8 ft (2 m or 2.4 m) high 'bushy' mess which you have to trim into shape to complete your obstacle. Steeplechase fence builders use pruners and secateurs to trim the birch, but if you lack patience you can attack it with a chainsaw.

Though the machine tends to smash the ends of the saplings where it cuts them, you can trim them afterwards with a pair of stout shears, and once the birch has weathered it looks attractive.

To cut off the top of the birch twigs neatly in a straight line, you will need a guide along which to run the chainsaw. Find a straight sawn fencing rail and tack it on to two stakes, which should be pushed into the frame or nailed on to the front of the frame, with the nail-heads left proud for easy removal afterwards with a jemmy. Use your measuring stick to set the guide rail at exactly the height at which you want the birch. When it is in the right position, run the chainsaw bar along the top of the rail and trim off the tops of the birch. The fence will look more attractive if you leave the equivalent of one bundle of birch uncut at either end of the fence. It is also better if you cut the top of the birch at an angle, making it higher on the landing side, but this requires considerable skill with the chainsaw. If you are unhappy about this method, it is better to make a good job of cutting it off square than an untidy job of cutting it off at an angle. When you have cleared away all the waste birch, use shears or pruners to trim the front and back, removing any whiskers that may be protruding. Finally, trim and tidy up the tops which you have left sticking up at either end.

☐ Do not stuff birch frames too much in advance of a competition. If cattle are likely to be in the field after you have built the obstacle, fence off the birch, otherwise they will almost certainly eat it. Once exposed to the elements, birch rots like any other timber. When green, the twigs are extremely supple and springy, but after a year the saplings will have been alternately wet and then dried out, and they will become brittle, breaking off when a horse brushes through the fence. For this reason, always check that year-old fences are in sound condition. You can prolong the life of the birch by keeping it covered, thus preventing it from getting wet when the fence is not being used.

☐ A fence can either be made using one or two frames as above, or an apron can be built on to the front of a frame. The easiest way of MAKING A BIRCH APRON is to lay the birch horizontally on top of bales of straw, but for safety the birch must be fixed securely. Stack the bales two to three deep in front of the fence in the form of steps, up to just below the top half-round rail. Using stakes, fix an additional half-round rail on the ground, immediately in front of the first row of bales; it is best to do this before you put the bales in place, but make sure that it is the right distance from the fence so that the bales will fit tightly into the gap. Then at 3 ft (1 m) intervals, attach lengths of No 8- or No 10-gauge soft galvanised wire *to the back* of the half-round rail. Secure it with one staple, the ends being bent back over that staple, with another one knocked in to lock it tight. Hold the lengths of wire out on to the ground on the take-off side of the fence so that they are out of your way. Then start to lay the bundles of birch on top of the bales. It is neater to have the bushy ends of the bundles facing the outside edges of the fence. This means that you

Bales in position and wires attached to the back of the half-round rail on the ground.

Laying the bundles on top of the bales.

The finished fence.

Straining tight the retaining wire on the back of the fence.

end up with all the butt ends of the birch in the middle, so you will have to open up several bundles of birch and lay individual saplings in alternate directions to hide the butt ends.

When you have completely covered the straw, you are ready to wire down the birch. Pass a length of wire over the top of the horizontal birch, underneath the top half-round rail, through the vertical birch and out on the other side. It is very difficult to thread the wire through the vertical birch, so it is advisable to make some sort of 'needle' out of a piece of $\frac{3}{8}$ in (approx 11 mm) steel rod with a hole in the end, which you can attach to the wire in order to pull or push it through the birch. Then use a pair of fencing pliers to lever the wire underneath the back rail. One man should strain the wire while the other jumps up and down on the birch in the front, or taps it down with a crowbar or sledgehammer. When you have pulled the wire as tight as you possibly can, secure it with two staples. Fix all the wires in the same manner, making sure that you pull them all to the same tension so that the birch on the front is even. You can then cut the strings on the bundles, pull out the strings, and trim the birch

Detail of the wire secured tightly on the back rail.

113

with shears to remove any whiskery bits. You will see the bales showing at either end of the fence. If you have left enough birch overhanging the ends, attach a piece of wire to the end of the half-round rail on the ground, fold the birch down over the ends of the bale, and secure it with the wire at the appropriate angle, on to the back post. Alternatively, you can square off the birch and plant instant Christmas trees against the ends of the fence to hide any bits of straw that may be showing. The fence should now look something like a steeplechase fence.

PORTABLE FRAMES. These fences are best bought from a recognised contractor whose tried and tested design will stand up to the rigours of both jumping and transportation. They come ready stuffed, and have an apron which moves around with them. If you want to make your own, study closely the design used by the professionals.

BULLFINCH. This is another type of fence for which birch is used. To build one, make a frame as for a simple upright birch fence, with half-round rails on either side of the posts. You can either stuff the birch tight as for a brush fence, or you can simply stick it loosely in the frame by hand. If you have stacked it and pulled it up tight, trim off the excess birch a bit at a time with pruners, to leave a screen through which it is just possible to see. If you are stuffing the frame by hand with individual saplings, continue until you have the required thickness of birch at the top. For a competition, you will always need a spare bundle of birch beside a bullfinch, to fill it if a hole appears, and to keep it the same throughout the day.

Bullfinch.

ARTIFICIAL BRUSH FENCE. You can make an attractive artificial hedge using bales of straw covered with spruce branches. First, build a standard post and rail fence, using a round top rail. Then nail on at least two lighter lower rails under the top rail. The spruce must always be lower than the top rail, which must show clearly. If a thick top rail is used it can reduce the height of the spruce, spoiling the look of the fence. To avoid this, use a half-round top rail instead. Cut off the tops of the posts at the correct height in a line with each other.

Frame of fence showing the stacked bales with the front row tipped up on end.

The fence ready for dressing, showing the curved shape of the front row of bales.

Weaving the small spruce branches into the strings of the bales.

Attaching the long branches to tie the fence together.

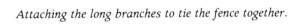

Cut them at an angle, so that they are 2 in to 3 in (5 cm to 8 cm) lower on the take-off side. If you have done it accurately you will be able to lay the half-round rail flat on top of these posts. Check that it is the correct height, then nail it securely on to the top of the posts. When sitting at this angle it will be quite strong. Again, fix lower rails on to the posts under it.

Stake a half-round rail on the ground at a distance equal to the required number of bale (straw) widths in front of the rails. This distance should be little more than the height of the fence, otherwise the fence will look too low and flat. Stack bales in a step fashion against your lower rails and out to the rail on the ground. The outermost row of bales should be stood up on end and curved slightly. You can bend a bale by putting your knee in the middle of it and pulling on either end until you have the required curve; the reason for doing this is to have the strings of the bales at the front, and to make an attractive curved shape. Proceed to weave small spruce branches in and out of the strings of the bale until all the bales are completely covered. At the top they can simply be laid on the bales. This method will help to tie the bales firmly together as well as holding the spruce in place.

When you have completely covered the front and top of the bales with the small spruce, select several long branches. Make a series of holes with a crowbar 12 in to 15 in (30 cm to 38 cm) apart between the front row of bales and the rail on the ground. Push the butt ends of the long branches into these holes as far as you can, then pass the branch over the bales and the spruce and underneath the top rail of

The completed fence.

the fence. The spruce should be tight up against the underside of the top rail, and it should be quite difficult to pass these long branches between it and the bottom of the rail. One member of the team should then pull on the end of the branches as hard as possible, while the other presses down on the front of the fence. When it has been pulled tight, the end of the branch can be secured with a nail or a staple either to the underside of the back top rail or to the next rail down. Continue along the fence in this manner.

Using ordinary garden shears, trim off any excess spruce which sticks out between the long branches.

Finally, tidy up the ends, which can be covered up by sticking the smaller bits of spruce into the ends of the bale. Use any offcuts of spare spruce to cover the back of the fence to hide the straw so that there is none showing anywhere. If you have done this correctly, as with the birch-covered bales, it will be strong enough to withstand a horse banking the fence. It will also be very attractive to look at, and will be even smarter if you stand Christmas trees at each end.

(i) Steeplechase Fences

These are made in one or two different ways. They are either the permanent type, with the birch set into a trench below ground level, or the portable type of fence built in sections, each in a timber frame 6 ft to 8 ft (1.8 m to 2.4 m) wide, and using two or three sections to make up one fence, which can be moved around from place to place quite easily.

Steeplechase fence, side view.

To build a permanent steeplechase fence you must first dig a trench the width of the fence, approximately 12 in (30 cm) deep and 18 in (46 cm) wide. Drive 3 in to 4 in (8 cm to 10 cm) diameter of square section stakes into the ground on either side of the trench, approximately 4 ft (1.2 m) apart. Then attach rails to the inside of the two rows of stakes. The rails should be roughly the same size as the stakes, and you should be able to nail them on satisfactorily. Fit two cross-pieces between the stakes at one end of the trench. The back rail should be approximately 30 in (76 cm) high and the front one 24 in (60 cm). Fill the frame in the same way as described before. When the entire frame is stuffed tightly, fit two cross-pieces to close the other end of the frame. This type of fence should definitely have the birch cut off at an angle, so that it is lower on the take-off side, sloping upwards to a higher landing side. To do this, you could fix a rail on both sides of the fence at the required height, then rest the bar of the chainsaw on either rail while using the machine to shape the birch. The other way of cutting off the tops is to use long-handled pruners or secateurs. First, stretch a rope or a string tightly across the top on both sides, and then cut accurately between the two lines.

□ To make an apron on this type of fence, lie birch bundles horizontally on the ground, coming out to about 3 ft (1 m) in front of the fence and almost as high as the top. Next, fix individual saplings into crowbarred holes approximately 3 in to 4 in (8 cm to 10 cm) apart all the way along the front edge of the fence. Secure them in place with a rail laid across them, approximately half-way up, then wire it back to the top rail. If the fence is very wide, you will need to tie down the rail, not only at the ends, but in one or two places at the centre, passing the wire through the birch. Level off the ends of these saplings with the top of the rest of the fence. You can then cover the apron with either spruce branches or gorse, to make the fence look attractive.

Portable steeplechase fence, viewed from the landing side.

(j) Ditches and Banks

NATURAL DITCHES are to be found in most parts of the countryside, and you will be unlucky if there are none on your course site. They vary considerably in dimension and shape, so before you incorporate any into a cross-country course, make sure that they are safe and suitable for the horses and riders who will be jumping them.

To use a natural ditch as an obstacle, either with a fence alongside or over it — or without a fence at all — the sides should be sloping, and the turf on either side must be well established and undamaged. If the sides are steep or pitted and worn away by livestock, or if a large number of horses will be jumping the ditch in wet conditions, its take-off edge will need some form of reinforcement. This can be achieved in some circumstances by fitting a take-off rail on the edge of the ditch. Alternatively, the ditch will have to be strongly revetted from the take-off edge right down to its base.

A TAKE-OFF RAIL OR POLE is sufficient only if the ditch is shallow and the slides are sloping. Choose a strong pole (preferably a treated one) such as a telegraph pole, 6 in to 8 in (15 cm to 20 cm) in diameter. Lay

Digging out the previously marked groove to the shape of the pole.

it on the ground 2 in to 3 in (5 cm to 8 cm) in front of the take-off edge of the ditch. When it is in position, use a spade to chop a mark in the ground all the way along both sides of the pole. Then remove the pole. Dig out a groove in the turf between the two marks, to a depth of approximately half the diameter of the pole. Replace the pole, and if it does not fit snugly, remove it and make adjustments to the shape of the groove as necessary. When the pole is in position there should still be enough earth between it and the ditch itself to ensure that the ground cannot become worn away, which might allow a horse's leg to slip underneath the pole and into the ditch.

Next take a crowbar to make pairs of pilot holes opposite each other on either side of the rail — one pair at each end and one in the middle. If the pole is more than 18 ft (5.5 m) long, a fourth pair of holes should be made. Drive into the holes half-round, treated fencing stakes, with their flat side against the rail. Square-sawn stakes could be used as an alternative. At this stage do not drive the stakes fully home. The length of the stakes will depend on the depth and softness of the ditch, but 3 ft (1 m) should suffice. Either $5\frac{1}{2}$ ft or 6 ft (1.65 m–1.8 m) stakes can be cut in half to make two. If you drive

The pole sitting neatly in the groove ready for staking.

Tightening the wire by tapping the stakes in further.

Squaring the edge of the bank to fit the sleepers.

in the pointed end of the stake first, you can then put another point on the top with a chainsaw before cutting it in half, so that the stake is held firmly. It is quite safe to cut the point without having to hold the stake with your foot.

Next cut a length of No 8-gauge or No 10-gauge soft wire, to loop round behind one stake, joining the two ends together behind the opposite stake, pulling them as tight as you can by hand. Staple the wire firmly to the stake. To tighten the wire, tap in the stakes with your sledgehammer or mall until the rail is forced hard down into the ground. When all the stakes have been driven in securely, there is no way in which the rail can be moved by a horse kicking it or treading on it, and you will have a safe, sound take-off for your ditch.

Revetting a Ditch

A ditch with steep sides or unsound banks will require revetting the whole way down on the take-off side. You should not revet on the landing side of a ditch, as this can injure a horse if it leaves its hind legs behind; a rider, too, can be badly hurt if flung against the revetting on the far side by a refusing horse. The best way to revet is to use railway sleepers or similar timber. First of all, consider how wide you want the ditch to be. Remember to include the width of the sleepers in the spread measurement. If the ditch is too narrow, you

Boring a hole to take the tie-back wires.

*Sleepers, stakes, and tension
tie-back wires, all in position.*

*Detail showing the tie-back wire
twisted so as to tighten it.*

124

may have to dig away the sides to fit the sleepers right down to the bottom. To make a fence inviting it is usually necessary to revet the ditch to a width of two sleepers.

Lay the first pair of sleepers in position at the required width in the bottom of the ditch, end to end. They may have to be dug in, so that when further sleepers are added, the top pair are flush with the top of the bank all the way along. To achieve this, measure up from the sleeper to a spirit level which is resting on the take-off bank. Measure down from the top edge of the bank to the sleepers at both ends and in the middle. These measurements should all be the same, and must allow for an equal number of sleeper heights.

Then, using a crowbar, make pilot holes in the ditch at either end of and in the middle of each of the sleepers. Drive a treated half-round or square-sawn stake into the crowbar holes, tightly against the outer edges of the sleeper. If the bottom of the ditch is soft and muddy, make sure that the stakes go in far enough to provide a firm anchorage. When the stakes are in position, lay the other sleepers on top of the bottom ones, until all but the top layer are in position. You can nail through the stakes into the sleepers to hold them temporarily, but be sure that they are in the correct position before you knock the nails fully home.

Opposite each stake dig a trench at least $3\frac{1}{2}$ ft (approx 1 m) back into the revetted bank, and approximately one spade's width and one sleeper deep. If the ground is soft and sandy you should consider making a longer trench to reach firmer ground. If possible, save the top layer of grassy turf to replace later. At the further end of the trench make a crowbar hole and drive in another treated stake. It is most important to use stakes that have been pressure-treated: when stakes rot there is no support at all for the revetting, and you will not be able to see that they have rotted.

When all the stakes are secured as firmly as possible, take a length of No 8-gauge soft wire and loop it round a tieback stake, then join the two ends to meet behind the opposite stake, passing them between the top and second layer of timbers. Join and staple the wires, as illustrated, pulling them as tightly as you can with a pair of fencing pliers. When you have done this for each stake along the length, twist the two wires together, using a small bar to tension the wire. Make sure that the wires are really tight, but if there is a gap behind the sleepers be careful that you do not pull them over in the process. When this has been done, the final two sleepers can be placed on top and nailed to the stakes. Cut off the tops of the stakes — flush with but angled slightly away from — the top of the sleepers, and then surform the rough edges. Carefully fill in any gaps between the sleepers and the bank, and also the trenches. When backfilling with soil, put in a layer of no more than 2 in to 3 in (5 cm to 8 cm) at a time, and thump it down very firmly with the end of a stake or with a purpose-made ground hammer. If you have kept the original turf, replace this on top, and the take-off will recover in the quickest possible time.

Attach the wires to the front of the stake and lock the ends down with additional staples.

Trim off the tops of the stakes at an angle. Note that regulations now require special safety trousers and gloves to be worn when using a chainsaw.

Back-filling and firming the ground behind the sleepers.

To reduce the width of a Ditch

The same method as above can be followed. Simply build up the sleeper revetting from the bottom of the ditch, the correct distance away from the landing side. You may then be left with a considerable gap to backfill. If necessary, fix extra sleepers or other timber at either end of the revetting to prevent the filling from falling round the side and into the ditch. It is always best to backfill a large gap with hardcore or stone. If you use earth, it can become very soft after rain, causing a dangerous take-off. Any type of hardcore will do as bulk to fill the deeper part of the hole. It can then be topped with soil or stone of approximately 1 in (25 mm) diameter graded down to dust. Do not tip large stones on to the wires, which could then stretch and become loose. Either give the wires some protection, or carefully build up stone around them by hand before tipping more hardcore on top.

If you have to make a ditch narrower it should always be the take-off side which is revetted. Also, try to avoid using any timber or reinforcement across the ditch either at or below ground level; if a horse should become trapped in the ditch, this could prevent him from getting out easily. Ideally, the horse should be able to walk along the bottom of a ditch until he finds a place where he can hop out without difficulty.

A deep, narrow ditch can be dangerous if a horse gets trapped in it. To reduce the depth, put a pipe, or pipes, in the bottom to carry

A ditch with both width and depth reduced by piping and revetting.

any water which may flow down the ditch, and then cover them with hardcore or stone.

If you do not have enough natural ditches on your site you can make them artificially.

Try to site ARTIFICIAL DITCHES in natural situations, such as the bottom of a hollow or in an existing fence line; ditches are never found on the crest of a hill. A ditch should be wider than the actual fence, as this will look much more inviting to the horse. Beware of making the ditch too shallow, although this is very tempting because of the hard work involved in digging and removing the soil. Always have it deep enough for a horse to realise what it is, so that it does not put its feet in the ditch and fall. The minimum depth for a ditch should be 1 ft (30 cm) although preferably it should be at least $1\frac{1}{2}$ ft (45 cm) deep.

The easiest way to dig a ditch is to use a mechanical back-hoe digging machine (see page 56). Use the arm of the digger at the side of the tractor, because if it is straight behind the tractor it will produce a ditch with sheer sides which will have to be revetted the whole way down. Using the arm at the side, a machine can dig a ditch with sloping edges which will require less work from you to make it safe to jump. Remember that the take-off pole or revetting must be included within the maximum spread measurement of the ditch, so do not dig it too wide initially. You can always widen it a little at a time, but if you make it too wide you can never replace the soil again in the same way.

The faces of drops, steps and banks can be reinforced by the same method as ditches. Usually these will need revetting to their full height, and again railway sleepers are ideal for this purpose. For drop fences where there is a considerable height of revetting to be supported, you may need to use longer and stouter vertical timbers rather than ordinary fencing stakes. Railway sleepers make excellent vertical supports; you may have to wire them half-way up as well as at the top. To hold the revetting very firmly in place, the tieback stakes should be placed well back into the bank up to 6 ft (1.8 m) or more, away. It is surprising how easily the considerable weight of earth behind the revetting can push it over.

Steps often need supporting at the sides as well as at the face. This looks neatest if the sides are revetted with the same materials as the face. They must be just as strong, as there is heavy pressure from the filling inside the steps pushing the timber outwards.

Revetting a Bank
Banks should be revetted on one or all of their sides. For an artificial box-shaped bank revetted on all four sides using standard $8\frac{1}{2}$ ft (2.6 m) sleepers, a convenient size to make the obstacle frame is two sleepers by one sleeper. This ensures a suitable distance for horses to jump on and off. Lay out the bottom rows of sleepers on the two long

The bottom row of sleepers laid in position.

Stakes driven in around three sides.

sides and at one end to start with. Make sure that the corners are square; to achieve this use the formula that a right-angled triangle has sides 3, 4 and 5. For instance, measure 3 ft (3 m) from the corner along one side and make a mark, then 4 ft (4 m) from the corner along the other side, and make a mark. When the distance in a straight line between the two marks is 5 ft (5 m), then the corner will be a right angle, or square.

The bottom line of sleepers may have to be dug in to the ground so that the top is at the required height. When the sleepers are in position, with the single end sleeper placed inside the sleepers on the long sides, drive in three stout supporting stakes per sleeper, all the way round. Nail through the stakes into the sleepers to hold them firm. Use 8 in (20 cm) nails to secure the sleepers together at the corners, then build up subsequent layers of sleepers until the required height is reached. Now by reversing your trailer or dumper into the gap you have left at the end, fill in most of the inside of the bank with hardcore or large stones. Be careful that it does not press outwards on the sides. If necessary, use temporary props for extra support. You should not fill it above the bottom of the top row of sleepers. Now position the sleepers and stakes across the open end of the bank. Next, with loops of wire, join each stake with the one opposite and strain the wire by twisting it with a bar through the middle. Use another length of wire to tie together the two stakes nearest to each corner, across all four of them. A corner is always the

Temporary props added to support the sides while filling with hardcore.

Tipping in the first load of hardcore.

Supporting wire attached below the uppermost sleeper on top of the hardcore.

131

Detail of the supporting wires across a corner.

Adding the top layer of small stone.

weakest part of the bank, and to prevent it from bulging outwards it is important to have the stakes held together very securely.

An alternative way of wiring the inside of the bank is to obtain an old car wheel from a scrapyard, put it in the middle of the bank and link it with wires, like spokes, to each stake. Then strain them tightly, carefully and evenly.

If you are filling the bulk of the bank with large hardcore you will have to position the rest of it underneath the wires by hand. Heavy lumps of stone or brick would stretch the wires if dropped on to them so that they become slack and ineffective. However, you could avoid this tedious process by using finer material, such as stone no larger than 2 in (5 cm) in diameter. If you tip this in carefully it should not affect the tension of the wires, although you must always check them to make sure, and if necessary tighten them up whilst you can still get at them.

Once the bank has been closed in on all four sides, to get the hardcore on to the bank you must either shovel it by hand from a trailer or dumper, or tip it in from the bucket on the front loader arm of the tractor or digger, or use the rear backhoe arm of a digging machine. The top 4 in to 6 in (10 cm to 15 cm) should be made up of approximately 1 in (2.5 cm) down to dust crushed stone. You will probably find that after a few weeks the stone will have settled and dropped down below the top of the sleepers, so that it will need topping up. To make the bank as firm as possible, and to save time,

One way to level the final layer.

Firming the stone with a vibrating compactor plate.

you can hire a vibrating compactor plate to run over the hardcore just above the wires, and then use it again on top of the final layer to press the stone down firmly, and bind the top surface, so that it is less likely to be moved by horses' feet.

If you want a grass-topped bank, there must be several months between the time of building it and the competition. You can either turf the top of the bank, or put a thin layer of soil on the top, compact it extremely firmly, and then sow it with grass seed. This is not recommended if the weather conditions are likely to be bad on the day of the competition and if there are a large number of horses expected to jump the fence. Remember, turf and grass seed will not grow during the winter, so either of these must be established in the spring or early summer for use the following autumn.

If you prefer, it is possible to hide the vertical supporting timbers on the inside of the revetting, in which case it will be necessary to drill a hole in each sleeper (or whatever you are using) before bolting them with $\frac{1}{2}$ in (13 mm) coach bolts to the vertical supports on the inside.

Another method of revetting, which also looks attractive, is to use vertical slats nailed on to a frame. First you will need lengths of treated timber, (railway sleepers are again ideal), to make vertical supports. Space them no more than 5 ft (1.5 m) apart along the length of the bank or steps and 2 ft (60 cm) approximately, into the ground. They should be wired back into the bank and securely fixed to tieback stakes. Wire or bolt two lines of horizontal timbers in front of them, or between them, at the top and half-way down. At the base, dig out a trench approximately 6 in (15 cm) deep and running the entire length of the fence. Obtain some half-round timbers, 3 in to 6 in (8 cm to 15 cm) in diameter, from a sawmill. They must have straight and parallel edges. Stand the half-round slats vertically, the bottom end in the trench, and then nail them securely to the horizontal supports.

If rustic timbers are used for this purpose they will rot eventually, in which case it is possible to lever them off, one at a time, and to replace them with new ones. Obviously, treated timber would last longer.

Slab wood or sawmill offcuts can be used as inexpensive alternative materials, but they have a short life and tend to look untidy.

When backfilling behind this type of revetting, make sure that the filling material is packed right down and goes underneath the lowest horizontal rail, otherwise it could eventually drop down, leaving subsidence or a bad hole at the top.

Revetted steps.

When building related steps, the proportions need very careful thought and plotting. Build the top step first so that the material from this can then be tipped down to fill the step below.

A three-sided step showing the bracing wires.

The bottom step in position. Note the additional revetting to support the bank at the sides.

Sleepers fitted together flush using coach screws through angled iron brackets.

Nailing half-round slats vertically to the front of the frame.

This method of construction makes an attractive fence.

(k) Water Obstacles

There are basically two types of water obstacles: those which a horse must clear by jumping *over* the water in one leap, and those which ask the horse to jump *into* the water.

☐ *Important* Any water obstacle must be built so that the horse will know whether it is supposed to clear the water or to jump into it.

☐ The maximum width that a horse should be asked to jump over water when going across country is about 12 ft (3.6 m); considerably less for Novice and Pony Club competitions.

The absolute minimum width of any existing water obstacle which a horse is expected to jump *into* should be 17 ft (5 m). *New* water obstacles should preferably be at least 26 ft (8 m) wide.

Any width of water between these two dimensions is extremely dangerous. On approach a horse may think he has to jump the obstacle in one, and in attempting to do so he could fail to clear it or could land wrongly against the far bank of the obstacle, which may result in a fall and injury.

☐ When a water obstacle which a horse should jump into is the minimum width of 17 ft (5 m), it is safe only if the horse is prevented from approaching too fast. By including a sharp turn or corner immediately before the fence, or another obstacle one or two strides in front of it, you can avert the danger of a horse trying to jump the whole thing in one. But if there is a long straight approach to the water with nothing to prevent a horse from galloping at it, a minimum of 26 ft (8 m) of water is recommended.

Open water fences, to be jumped from bank to bank, can either be built over a natural stream or ditch, or dug out artificially from the side of a lake or pond. They will almost certainly require some form of revetting on the take-off side, as it is most important that this type of fence has a sound take-off.

☐ If an obstacle is to be filled with water only for the duration of the competition, you must ensure that it does not soak into the surrounding, making the take-off or landing side of the fence soft. It does not matter if the ditch is quite deep and there is only a little water in the bottom. However — particularly when the water level is close to the top — it will be necessary to make the banks firmer. You will have to dig out the take-off to a depth of 1 ft to $1\frac{1}{2}$ ft (30 cm to 46 cm) below water level and 4 ft to 6 ft (1.2 m to 1.8 m) back from the edge of the water; remove the soil; and replace it with stones or hardcore in the bottom and 1 in or $\frac{3}{4}$ in (25 mm or 18 mm) to dust stone on the top.

☐ The landing side of an open water must never, under any circumstances, be revetted, because a horse failing to clear the spread or leaving his hind legs behind will injure himself on the revetting timbers. It should be a gradual slope up out of the water, until the bank meets ground level on the other side. You may also need to make up the landing with stone, to prevent it becoming too soft, so that a horse who makes a mistake or jumps short has a good firm landing in or out of the water, and does not hurt himself.

A course builder often pays heavily for a mistake made in the construction of a water obstacle into which a horse has to jump. The most usual cause of trouble, for both horses and riders, is an unsound base. As well as its obvious danger, it is also a waste of the course-builder's time, materials and, in some cases, machinery hire.

A water obstacle is constructed either from a natural stream or pond, or from an artificial hole dug in the ground and sealed to keep the water in. On a cross-country course the former is preferable, as a natural obstacle usually fits in better with the surroundings and appears more inviting. Some streams and shallow rivers have firm gravel bases which are sound enough to support numerous horses jumping in and out and crossing them without deteriorating in any way. To be certain that the base is absolutely sound, and that it will be safe for the duration of the competition, arrange for one or two riders to trot or canter their horses through the stream as many times as possible. If the obstacle passes this test and does not break or sink anywhere, and if it is wide enough, it should be suitable just as it is, with a fence built on the take-off or landing side to your own choice. If you need to widen the stream or river you may find that the gravel base does not extend beneath the existing banks. If so, it will be necessary to construct a new base to the area which is widened, as in any other case 'on land'.

☐ Ponds and lakes are less likely to have a natural hard bottom, and even if they do it will usually be covered with a thick layer of soft, silty mud. To make the obstacle safe, any layer of mud, clay, or soft earth must be removed from the bottom and replaced with sound hardcore.

☐ It is virtually impossible to construct a sound base to a water obstacle while the water remains in it. To be sure that you have removed all soft mud and replaced it with a good, level, firm layer of hardcore, it is essential to pump out, or bypass, the water away from the area where you are working. For ponds or small lakes it is relatively easy to hire a pump and remove the water into the nearest ditch or into a nearby field. Do not take the pump away until you are sure that the pond does not fill up again overnight.

It is possible to evacuate the water from a short length of slowly flowing stream. To do this, build a dam upstream from the area where you intend to work. If you have a big enough pump, it should be possible to direct the water from the upstream side of your dam to below where the obstacle will be, in order to keep the water out. You may have to build another smaller dam on the downstream side of your working area to stop the water flowing back into it from below. You will have to leave the pump running all the time, including overnight, to prevent the area from becoming flooded.

Another way to achieve the same objective is to pipe the water from one side of your work area to another.

When draining areas of wet ground, contractors often use long lengths of flexible, corrugated plastic pipe. The ideal equipment for the job is a pipe *without slots*. It can be obtained in diameters of up to

6 in (15 cm) in long rolls of approximately 164 ft (50 m). If the volume of water is more than can be taken by a 6 in (15 cm) pipe, simply double up and use two or more pipes, as required.

Build the dam far enough upstream from your area of work to allow the pipes to lie on the banks either side of where you are going to build your obstacle, so that they are out of the way. Alternatively, lie the pipes in the bottom of the stream and move them from side to side as you work. It is possible for one man to move the pipe, either by levering it with a crowbar or simply lifting it while the water is still running through it.

You may find it useful to leave the pipe in the bottom of the obstacle and to build the base over the top of it. If it stays there, you can then divert the water through the pipe at any time to dry out the area which you are using. You will then be able to make sure that the base is still sound, that there are no objects which could be dangerous lying in the bottom, and that no unwanted layer of mud has built up over the base.

When you have successfully dried out the area where you intend to work, you can start preparations on the base itself. You will invariably find that some sort of mechanical digging machine is essential. First scoop out all the sludge at the bottom. If no hard layer

Removing the soft sludge down to a drier and firmer layer.

is found under the mud, continue to dig down until you are 15 in to 18 in (38 cm to 46 cm) below the actual depth at which the base of the water should be. If it is still too soft and wet at this depth, continue to dig. If it appears that you are never going to reach a reasonably dry layer, you should consider using some form of barrier, to prevent the mud mixing with your eventual layers of hardcore. When building roads, engineers use a material such as terram, which is like a roll of thick blanket and can be laid underneath the layers of hardcore. It prevents the mud from working its way up into the hardcore and eventually making it soft. When using terram, simply roll it out over the area to be made up, and cover it with the first layers of hardcore. Begin with large hardcore — for example 6 in (15 cm) diameter stones, brick rubble, or broken-up concrete, which can often be obtained from demolition sites. If you are buying stone from a quarry, ask for it to be delivered 'clean', which means only large stones, without smaller stones or dust included. It is vital that there should be no earth, soft dust or mud mixed with the hardcore, as when mixed with water it becomes like 'pudding'.

The machine which removes the mud can also be used for spreading the hardcore over the entire base. If the machine cannot reach all the way across the obstacle area from the bank, you will

Laying the first layer of large hardcore.

have to work in strips, a piece at a time. Dig out the mud as far as the machine can reach from its position on the bank, and replace it by tipping in the hardcore to a depth of 10 in to 12 in (25 cm to 30 cm) and levelling it out. Be careful to avoid pushing the hardcore too close to the mud which is left. Drive the machine on to the hardcore which you have just laid, then dig out whatever mud you can reach from there, replacing it with hardcore. Level this, as before, then drive on to it, and so on, until you have completed the whole area. If the arm of the machine only swings through 180° you will probably have difficulty getting rid of the mud on to the bank behind you. You can either pile some of it on top of your dam at one end or the other, to make that larger, or use a four-wheel drive dumper — which can usually be manoeuvred on to the hardcore beside the digger — and fill this with the mud which is being removed.

If the base which you build for horses to jump on to and to go across is not sound enough to support the weight of a digger or tractor, it will not be sound enough to support horses, so do not be afraid of driving your machinery on to it.

When you have completely covered the area with a layer of large hardcore, you are then ready to put in the next layer. If you still have some depth to make up (more than 6 in or 15 cm), you might want to

Tipping in the middle layer.

fill this with an intermediate layer of material, which is approximately 2 in (5 cm) in diameter and should be clean and dust free. Spread this all over, to within a depth of 4 in to 6 in (10 cm to 15 cm) below the eventual level required. At this stage it is worthwhile to compact the hardcore in some way, either by using the tracks of the digger itself or a vibrating roller or compactor plate, which will seal the surface of the hardcore and ensure that it is really firm and level.

You will now be ready to put in the final surface of stone on to which the horses will actually jump. It should be either 1 in or $\frac{3}{4}$ in (25 mm or 18 mm) down to and including dust. Before you add this layer make sure that no water has crept back in while you have been working. If it has, pump it away. Spread out the layer of stone to cover the entire area, making sure that it finishes up at the required level. Remember that water always lies absolutely horizontal, so if you want the water to be the same depth all over, the layer of stone must also be horizontal. To achieve this, you could mark the bank with pegs at the water's normal level before the water is removed, which will help to ensure that your stone is the right height everywhere. Again, compress this layer firmly with the tracks of your digger or a vibrating roller or compactor plate. The dust when wetted and then allowed to dry afterwards will act like a mild

Levelling out the middle layer of hardcore.

Compacting the middle layer using caterpillar tracks. Alternatively, a vibrating roller or compactor plate can be used.

The final layer of small stone levelled and compacted.

cement and will set to form a crust. It will give you an absolutely firm surface, on to which horses may jump safely. Although they will not sink into it at all, their feet will be able to get a grip on it.

If you are intending to raise the water level above where it lies naturally, you may find that it will soak back into the banks on the take-off and landing sides of the fence, making them soft and wet. Always remember that where horses leave water they carry a considerable amount of it out with them, and the bank soon becomes wet and poached. If either of these cases applies, you may have to reinforce the banks by the same methods as above, as far up as necessary, to make sure that they do not become soft.

If there is no suitable natural water on your course site, you can build an artificial obstacle. The amount of work involved in its construction will depend on the type of soil where you intend to build it. A hole dug in heavy clay will often fill up with water naturally, and the water will be retained, whereas lighter, free-draining soils will absorb any water poured in them and it will soak away. The only way to discover whether your soil will hold water is to dig a test hole in the place where you intend to build the obstacle, fill it with water and see what happens. When building an artificial water obstacle, remember that it will have to be near a source of water. It will take a long time to fill it up from a $\frac{1}{2}$ in (13 mm) hose pipe, and any leaks (which eventually are inevitable) may prevent the flow of the hose pipe from reaching its destination. If you find that water stays in your test hole long enough to be suitable for a competition, all you need to do is to dig out the hole to the required size, 15 in to 18 in (37 cm to 45 cm) deeper than intended for the final depth, and fill the bottom with hardcore in the same way as for a natural pond. At least one side of the obstacle must slope up gradually, from the bottom, out on to dry land. This will make it easy to carry in the hardcore and to maintain the base in the future. It will also mean that a horse which gets into trouble in the water can get out again easily. Remember, also, to make the ground firm with hardcore for a suitable distance up the slope beyond the water, to prevent it becoming soaked.

If your test hole proves not to hold water, and you still want to make a water obstacle, you will have to line it to keep the water in. One way to do this is by using concrete. You will have to line not only the entire bottom of the obstacle, but also the sides to above where the eventual intended water level will be. The concrete must be laid so that it has no cracks between the bottom and the sides. At the sloping end you need to dig out a considerable depth and distance into the bank, so that the concrete ends above the water level yet still below a layer of small hardcore which protects the horses from direct contact with the concrete. If the concrete comes right up to ground level you will have to guard it with timber anywhere that you expect a horse to jump in or out.

Before the concrete has set hard, push lengths of $\frac{1}{2}$ in (13 mm) threaded rod, or 'studding' as it is sometimes called, into the top of the wet concrete at intervals around the edge, thus leaving the concrete slightly below ground level. When it has set hard, you can then fit timbers, with holes drilled in them, (probably railway sleepers) over the threaded rod, and put nuts on the end, set into counter-sunk holes, to hold them firm. If you allow the concrete to harden without doing this, you will have great difficulty in anchoring any timber on it, and you may have to drill the concrete, which is extremely difficult.

Alternatively, you can concrete only the bottom, and use this as a foundation on which to lay concrete blocks to help seal the sides. As it is almost essential to have a sloping end where horses can walk in or out easily, at this point you will have to be very careful how you connect the blocks to the concrete floor. Again, you will need to fit timbers on top of the blocks, where the horses will jump in or out. The concrete floor should be covered with 4 in to 6 in (10 cm to 15 cm) or 1 in or $\frac{3}{4}$ in (25 mm or 20 mm) down to dust stone. This will be the same material as used for a natural water obstacle. It is ideal for horses to jump on to, and will protect them from the concrete. This is an extremely expensive way of building a large water obstacle, but if you do it correctly it should be guaranteed to hold water and to last for many years — though it may never look natural.

It is impossible to seal water into a hole in the ground simply by using ordinary polythene sheeting. The sheeting is likely to become punctured when walked on, and the sharp edges of the stone which you have to tip on it will almost certainly puncture it. The only sheeting suitable for this job is made of special heavy-duty butyl rubber. It can generally be obtained from firms specialising in sheets for commercial vehicles, and they should be able to join pieces together to almost any shape or size that you may require. You should dig out your hole, approximately 12 in to 15 in (30 cm to 38 cm) deeper than the eventual bottom required.

The revetting for any steps or drops into water should be carried out first, before fitting the sheet. The butyl rubber should be strong enough not to be punctured by ordinary soil, but as you cannot be certain that there are no sharp stones or other items on the floor of the hole, it would be a wise precaution first to cover the whole area with a layer of soft builder's sand under where the sheet is to lie below the water level. The sheet must obviously extend underground far enough into the banks where there is a sloping entrance or exit to the water, so that the edge of the sheet is buried yet still higher than the eventual water level. It will have to go up against the front of the revetting and be tacked carefully to it, again above water level.

To make a tidy job, and for safety reasons, it is best to place the uprights which hold the revetting on the dry land side of the horizontal timbers. If this is the case, it may be necessary to bolt the timbers to the uprights. This enables the sheeting to fit flush against the flat timber face. You can then hide it by nailing vertical battens (e.g. sawmill offcuts) on to the face of the timber covering the sheet.

147

These can extend right to the bottom, below the water line, but should have nails driven through them only above the water line.

When the sheet is in place, first cover it with a layer of soft sand approximately 4 in (10 cm) deep, (or possibly soft limestone dust), then a layer of no less than 6 in (15 cm) of 1 in or $\frac{3}{4}$ in (25 mm or 20 mm) down to dust stone on top of the sand, laid carefully, and vibrated to make it really firm. This should provide a sound base to the obstacle and should give you a strong layer which will protect the sheet from being punctured. Drain the water from the obstacle regularly to ensure that this layer is not becoming worn away, thus allowing horses to get too close to the sheeting. Obviously if they do, it will very quickly become punctured and you will lose the water.

☐ To control the depth of water in an artificially built water obstacle (usually 6 in to 12 in or 15 cm to 30 cm but depending on the standard of competition) fill it to the required level and make sure that you have a reserve supply of water to top it up should any leaks occur. Remember that horses carry out a considerable amount of water with them, and this may need to be replaced.

☐ To control the depth of water in a pond you must locate the overflow or outflow from it, which is usually into a stream or ditch, but could be into a pipe. If no obvious overflow can be found, you will have to rely on pumping the water either in or out, to adjust the level. Where the pond flows out into a ditch or stream you can simply build a dam, using a pile of earth, mud, or timber, across the entrance to the ditch, to increase the height of the water in the pond. If the pond flows out into a pipe you may be able to block the end of the pipe, but make sure that you can also *un*block it easily. Otherwise the water level may rise too high, particularly if there is a lot of rain. A more accurate way of controlling the level is to obtain a short length — 2 ft to 3 ft (60 cm to 90 cm) — of corrugated plastic land drainage pipe (without slots). This should be attached to the end of the existing pipe, and must, therefore, be of similar diameter. Make sure that no water can leak through the joint. This can be achieved by using a section from an old tyre inner tube, stretched over the ends of the pipe and clamped tight with wire or large jubilee clips. The water will then flow out of the pond at whichever height you set the end of the pipe. Thus you have unlimited adjustment of the water level.

The level of running water can be controlled either by dams, sluices or, again, flexible pipes. Raising the level by damming it slows down its flow and causes a deposit of silt which may build up considerably in a short time. To prevent this, it is always advisable to remove the dam and to allow the water to flow at its natural level when the obstacle is not in use. It is better still to bypass the water away from the obstacle area altogether and to keep it completely dry, so that you can inspect the bottom and make sure that it remains safe. It is obviously not practical to do this with large or strongly flowing streams or rivers, but whenever it is possible for the flow of the river to be taken by one or two 6 in (15 cm) diameter pipes, it is well worth doing. Simply lay the pipe underneath the hardcore, make a dam of mud or earth at both ends of the obstacle, and bypass the water through the pipe. When you want to allow water back into the area, block off the entrance to the pipe on the upstream side. The water will gradually build up until it flows over the dam and starts to fill the area required. If you leave a suitable length of pipe protruding beyond the lower dam you can raise this up and prop it on a forked stick or something similar, to control the depth of the water. Alternatively, you could put another pipe through the lower dam or cut a groove in the lower dam to let the water flow out of the obstacle when it reaches the required level.

Remember that you will also need a small drainpipe passing through the lower dam at base level, to drain water from the obstacle when you have finished using it.

Where larger volumes of water must be retained, it is best to use some form of sluice. When the sluice is fully open it must always be wide enough to allow through the maximum amount of water which could flow down the stream without causing any blockage.

To build a sluice, dig a trench approximately one spade wide and slightly deeper than the bottom, across the stream and 12 in to 18 in (30 cm to 46 cm) into the bank on either side. Next set a stout piece of timber, such as a railway sleeper, into the bottom of the trench. You may have to hold it there temporarily to prevent it floating away. Drive two pairs of stout stakes into the bed of the stream up against the timber about three-quarters of the width of the stream apart. Between the stakes and the ends of the trenches, nail shorter lengths of timber similar to the one across the bottom. Replace the earth on either side of the timbers in the trenches and thump it down firmly. Nail a piece of 4 in × 2 in (10 cm × 5 cm) timber or half-round rail across the top of the timbers from bank to bank to strengthen the whole structure. It is now a simple matter to slot boards, or better still a piece of plywood, into the gap in the middle to shut off the

Fence in water. The rail shows clearly above the water level and any bow wave can pass easily underneath it.

water. If necessary, use mud to seal off any leaks should the flow not be sufficient to keep pace with them. Let the water flow over the board to gauge the water level, but do not let it flow over the bank at the side of the dam as it will quickly erode this away.

Obstacles in Water

For these fences you may have to put posts in before the bottom is built up. Otherwise, large blocks or trestles will be needed to support the fence; they should also be staked as securely as possible.

Any part of a fence to be jumped in water must always be built above water level, so that the wave made by a horse passes harmlessly underneath and does not bounce back at him as he is about to take off.

Obstacles into Water

Avoid large drops or spreads into water. Suitable types of obstacles include steps, logs, sloping fences, or a plain drop without a fence.

Fences out of Water

It is preferable to have one sloping side to all water obstacles. If a fence is built on the far bank, a plain step up is most usual, but a log then a step may be added, or similar. Do not have upright obstacles.

Fences into and out of water.

Options, Alternatives and Combinations

Any cross-country obstacle which offers a choice of two or more negotiable routes gives the rider an 'option' or 'alternative'. They are relatively new in eventing, but it has now become essential in international competitions to provide some easier options and alternatives to enable the less qualified competitors to get round.

The purpose of offering the rider a choice at either a single obstacle or at an obstacle complex may be:

1. To accommodate horse/rider combinations with varying standards of experience, training and skill on the same course,

and/or

2. To sort out the better horse/rider combinations without eliminating others,

and/or

3. To require all competitors to carefully analyse each obstacle (and the questions it asks) before tackling it,

and/or

4. To make the obstacle more interesting, for both competitors and spectators.

When building an option or alternative it is essential for a course designer to have a clear idea of what he is trying to achieve. The obstacle must be appropriate to the standard of the horses and riders who will be jumping it. On the one hand you should provide obstacles which are demanding enough to test the best horse/rider combinations; on the other you should not undermine the sport by eliminating the less able; and because of this the easier but longer alternative is important at international level. To achieve a satisfactory result, the 'easy' route should take *at least* 5 seconds longer (the equivalent of 40 metres or 43 yards) than the more difficult route.

151

OPTIONS

THE SIMPLEST FORM OF OPTION is a single obstacle on level ground which is basically uniform in design but offers a choice of either a straight or angled approach. Typical examples of this are 'snake' fences (zig-zag rails), shark's teeth, or echelon rails.

ANOTHER TYPE OF OPTION is a simple obstacle sited on undulating terrain, where a rider can choose between taking the higher or wider place which has an inviting approach, or a lower, easier section with a more difficult approach. Examples might be a simple log, or a post and rails on a slope.

A THIRD TYPE OF OPTION is a single fence designed to offer the rider two or more completely different obstacles of similar composition and in the same 'fence line'. One example is a telegraph pole set at a slight angle over a ditch, which gives a three-way choice (ditch to pole, pole to ditch, or over the point where the pole crosses the ditch).

Option. This obstacle does not offer any really different alternative routes but it does give the rider a choice of approach lines: i.e. to the right of an apex, to the left, or at an angle.

□It is important to try to ensure that the options at any single obstacle or complex are evenly balanced, particularly if the different routes through or over them involve approximately the same distance. It is a waste of time, effort and money to build an option if nobody is going to jump it. It is extremely difficult to predict what percentage will take the second route: so much will depend on the light, the weather, the footing, the attitude of the competitors during the course walk, the advice given by trainers, and how early riders in the competition fare. To the course designer, it is invaluable if the fence judges keep a record of just how many competitors went which way.

ALTERNATIVES

An 'option' becomes an 'alternative' when two or more completely different types of test are incorporated in the same obstacle. It usually takes the form of a straightforward but more imposing element, and an easier part (alternative), which takes longer. This has the extra advantage that in a competition a horse refusing at the more difficult part of the obstacle can then attempt the easier, slower alternative at his second, or third, attempt, thus perhaps avoiding elimination.

□A good alternative will provide a well-balanced choice, to satisfy and challenge both the competitor who is ready to upgrade his horse and the competitor who is taking part in his first Event at this level. The course designer will be happy if each possible option, or alternative, is used by a similar number of riders.

□At any competition easier than an official Preliminary (Novice) Event, only the simplest of alternatives should appear. The course designer must always be aware of the level of training of the horse and the experience of the rider. He should not assume that competitors at these lower levels appreciate the significance of the various options. For example, it would be inappropriate to ask an inexperienced rider to decide between jumping the corner or the two elements of a 'V'. At the Preliminary (Novice level), however, a choice between a direct or a slightly longer route, one jumping effort or two, becomes useful. The rider with the less experienced horse can take the two simpler elements, while the rider who wants 'to move his horse up' can take the corner.

□The cross-country speeds required at the lower levels (particularly in the United States where Novice runs at 350 mpm, Training from 400 to 450 mpm, Preliminary from 450 to 520 mpm and Intermediate from 520 to 550 mpm) are, relatively speaking, very slow. It is therefore hardly worthwhile to incorporate alternatives specially designed to penalise with time faults the rider who takes the longer but easier route. A fast horse can take the easiest route the whole way, jumping the long, simple alternatives, yet can still make the time and possibly even win, without ever tackling the intended tests. This situation should be avoided at any level. It is not until

Mary Young

153

speeds of 550 mpm and over are reached that short/difficult, long/easy alternatives become truly viable. This applies to Novice Horse Trials (525 mpm) and above, in Great Britain. However, if route B takes only one or two seconds longer than route A, it is a waste of effort. The time difference should be at least 5 seconds, and the rider's judgement of pace now becomes increasingly important.

A good course should incorporate seven basic types of obstacle: verticals, spreads, banks, drops, ditches, water, and brush fences (the last five make a cross-country course different from a show jumping course). A true cross-country horse should be able to negotiate all seven of these types of obstacle, so any option which incorporates one or more of them should not offer an alternative route which either avoids or circumvents the need for negotiating a specific test. In other words, if an obstacle complex includes a bullfinch (brush) on one route, it should include a bullfinch on the other. If it includes a drop on one route, it should include a drop on the other. Jack Le Goff puts it this way: 'If there is a water jump, I don't want to give the horse the option of not getting his feet wet.'

Another type of alternative is one increasingly used on more

Option fence with a choice of three routes:
(a) Rail followed by ditch.
(b) Ditch followed by rail.
(c) Rail and ditch combined in one effort.

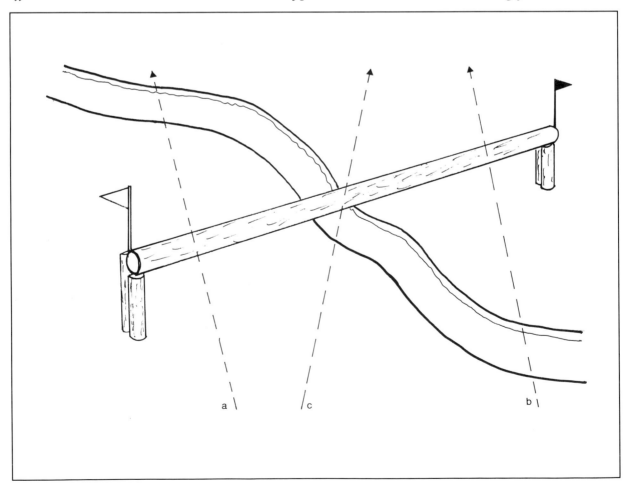

sophisticated courses; the 'escape route'. This applies chiefly to combinations. If a horse has a stop at a difficult and technical obstacle, why ask him to give it another try — particularly if either the approach or the landing present a problem or if it is uncomfortably close to a previous jumping element? After such a stop, the horse is almost surely out of the prize money — so why not provide him with an easier alternative which is incorporated in the same basic test, whatever it may be, but which does not require the horse to retackle an obstacle where he has already failed? This is not usually the kind of alternative that a rider will head for on his first try. In fact, it often is not really viable until one or more of the jumping elements of the complex have already been negotiated. An example here might be a vertical, set at a bounce distance at the top

Oxer or short vertical rails. The left-hand side appears more formidable, as it is built to maximum height and spread, but it is clearly-defined, broad, and slightly sloping. This may be preferable to the right-hand-side single rail which, although considerably smaller and less demanding, requires a more careful and accurate approach.

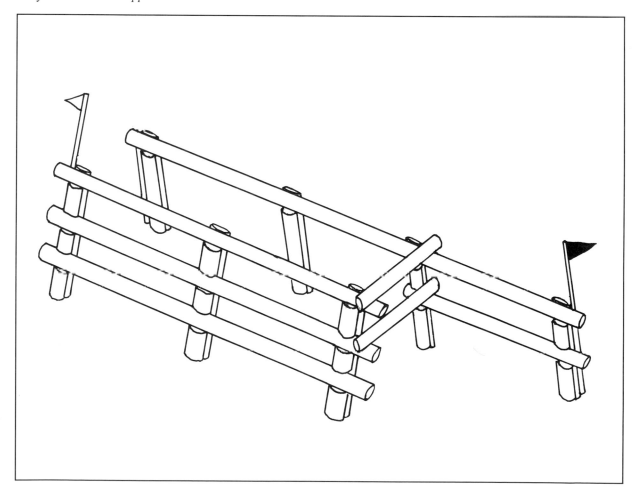

of three steps or banks up. If the horse goes up the three steps and then refuses the vertical — instead of having him go all the way down the three steps and up again, why not make it possible for him to jump an alternate panel either to the right or to the left of the one set on the direct line through?

Alternative. This obstacle was designed so that taking the easier route would cost the rider time. The direct route was called for between the right-hand cupola and the small tree to the left where the height was from over maximum to just maximum dimensions. The oxer became gradually narrower (less spread) towards the left. To the left of the left-hand cupola was a simple vertical. The further it was taken to the left, the further off was the direct route, the more time it took, and the more time penalty points were incurred.

COMBINATIONS

Any obstacle which involves more than one jumping effort in quick succession, so that each element is a component of an overall test, is called a combination. Like many simple, single obstacles, there may be only one route to choose when jumping a combination, or there may be a variety of options or alternatives offered by the course designer. An example of a simple combination is a one stride in and out where the elements are obviously related, one to the other.

The purpose of combinations on a cross-country course is to introduce particular tests that cannot be presented by a single obstacle. They are used:

1. To reproduce natural situations which might be encountered either riding across country or following hounds in the hunting field, such as jumping up on to a lane out of a field, turning sharp left down the lane, then sharp right over a gate off the lane, or jumping into and out of water, or going down a sleep slope, over a ditch at the bottom, then up a gentle slope and over a paddock fence into a field.

2. To test the rider's ability to judge the best place to jump, with a particular horse, taking into account his experience, and the terrain, conditions, light, etc.

3. To test the rider's ability to present his horse at the appropriate speed and in the correct outline and balance for the task in hand, thus demonstrating his obedience, and accuracy.

4. To test the horse's agility and boldness.

5. To entertain spectators with performances which are often more spectacular than those that take place over single element obstacles.

Remember that when designing a combination, safety is a priority, and an escape route must be provided so that a horse when refusing at one element can be extricated without jumping.

Courses at lower levels should be designed with the primary objective of educating rather than testing the horse. At the higher levels, though education is still important the emphasis is more on testing. At lower levels, therefore, combinations should be limited to only one or two, with simple, straightforward jumping efforts set at natural striding distances (24 ft to 26 ft or 7.5 m to 8 m, 36 ft to 38 ft or 11 m to 11.5 m, 48 ft to 50 ft or 14.5 m to 15 m, etc.), one from another, on relatively flat ground with good 'galloping' approaches. If set at an angle to each other they should be sited on a gentle, smooth curve of generous radius. At this early stage, neither horse nor rider should be asked to be too accurate — the fence must allow enough margin of error to allow for inexperience.

At higher levels, where the horse can rightfully be expected to have mastered a whole host of skills, technical questions can be introduced which test his ability to turn between the jumping elements of an obstacle; to extend and/or shorten his stride; to

157

negotiate obstacles either going up or down a slope or up and down a bank; to show boldness by jumping 'blind' (as through a bullfinch); to accelerate and/or decelerate between jumping efforts; to jump an obstacle at a specific point (as in negotiating a corner), and so on. It is here that we are examining the horse's agility; the rider's judgement of pace; the degree of collection and/or impulsion which the horse and rider together are able to achieve; the horse's and rider's ability to stop and to turn and to hold a chosen line without veering one way or the other, and so on.

The number of combinations which could be designed is almost infinite. Just think of the many ways in which you could combine the seven basic obstacle types into two, three and four element combinations. The only limitations are the variety of natural features available, the supply of building materials, construction techniques and, needless to say, the ingenuity and imagination of the course

This may be jumped in one leap over the smaller upright on the left, which has a big drop, or in two leaps on the right, by jumping over the higher upright rails on to a narrow platform and bouncing down a drop. The left-hand option is slightly easier, but involves a longer route round a diversion.

builder. However endless the possible permutations, there are a number of *general principles* which should be kept in mind in designing a combination:

1. The degree of difficulty of the combination and the particular technical question or questions which it will ask are determined by the experience of the riders and the horses, along with what you expect that they will achieve. At lower levels keep all combinations simple and straightforward, on relatively level ground with long, direct approaches, natural striding between elements, and incorporating only gentle turns. At higher levels:

(a) Prominent terrain features can be involved.
(b) Jumping elements incorporating tests of boldness can be introduced.
(c) Horses may be required to negotiate an obstacle at a specific point.
(d) Distances between elements can play a major role.
(e) Turns both into and through complexes can be more severe.

2. Whatever the level, care must be taken not to construct combinations which are either too tricky or too trappy and which therefore tend to discourage a horse. What you don't want is a good horse to have a bad experience — rather, you want to reward the big, free-going, bold jumper for taking the complex with impulsion, courage, fluidity and grace. Remember that it is better to ask for a longer than normal rather than a shorter than normal stride between jumping elements. To have to jerk a horse up short in the middle of an obstacle complex accomplishes very little and looks cruel and ugly. Any test which requires excessive athletic ability or agility on the part of either the horse or the rider is bound to result in costly mistakes. Avoid extremes, and keep the questions at a level which the well-conditioned, well-prepared and well-trained horse, ridden intelligently, can reasonably be expected to master. Ask yourself: 'How will the best horses jump this?' and always try to ensure that the good horse and rider will have a happy experience, whatever the level.

3. Each of the jumping elements of a combination should be constructed either out of the same material or out of materials that resemble or complement each other. Like all the other obstacles on the course, they should be constructed from impressively massive materials. There is nothing less pleasing aesthetically than an obstacle complex where one rail is of pressure-treated pine and another of shag bark hickory, one post an old railroad tie (sleeper) and another a Cyprus log, and one bank revetted with landscape timbers and another with telephone poles. There are occasions when the course designer may want to use less massive materials, either to create an artistically desirable effect or purposely to introduce an airy appearance to an obstacle, but the general rule of thumb still

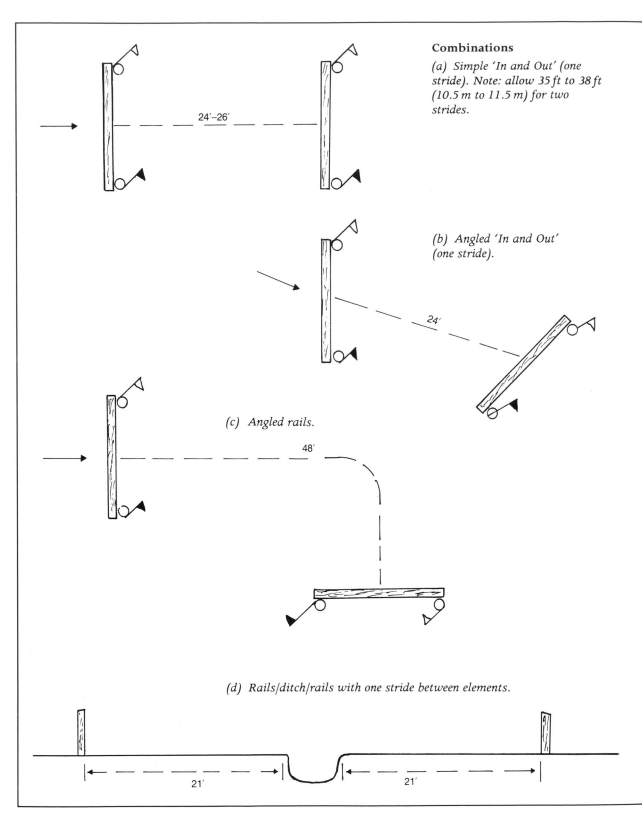

Combinations

(a) Simple 'In and Out' (one stride). Note: allow 35 ft to 38 ft (10.5 m to 11.5 m) for two strides.

24'–26'

(b) Angled 'In and Out' (one stride).

24'

(c) Angled rails.

48'

(d) Rails/ditch/rails with one stride between elements.

21'   21'

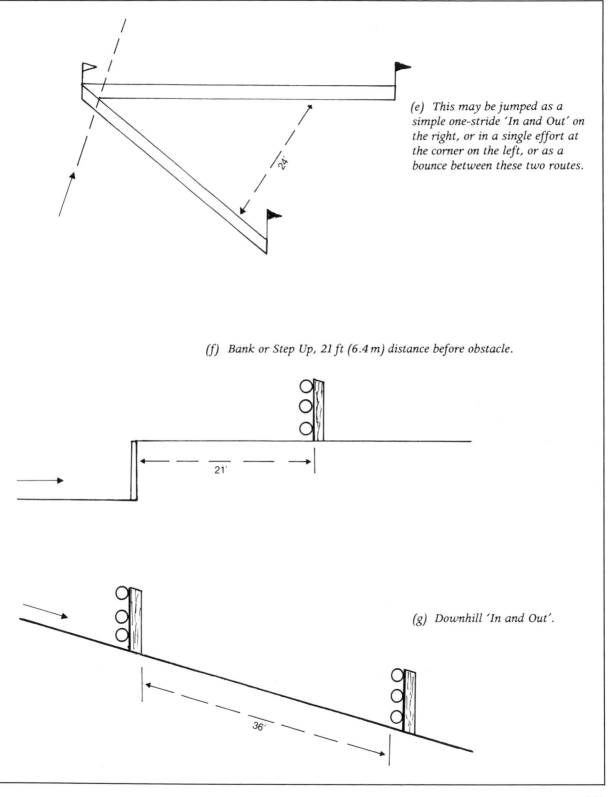

(e) This may be jumped as a simple one-stride 'In and Out' on the right, or in a single effort at the corner on the left, or as a bounce between these two routes.

(f) Bank or Step Up, 21 ft (6.4 m) distance before obstacle.

(g) Downhill 'In and Out'.

prevails: 'The bigger the posts and the rails, the safer the obstacle and the better the horse will jump it.'

4. A great deal of thought should be given to the siting, positioning, and orientation of all obstacle complexes. Generally speaking, combinations should be designed for the middle three-quarters of the course. In a course of 24 obstacles, this would mean after obstacle 3 and before 22. What you want is to get the horses going over some fairly conventional, straightforward and inviting fences before facing them with their first technical problem. Then, once they've conquered the major part of the course, bring them home smoothly. It is important, however, to put a combination towards the end to help to ensure that the rider has reserved the necessary energy and can show that over the last few fences, he still has left some balance and control.

Thought should also be given to locating combinations where they can be easily viewed by spectators. They are, after all, generally the most interesting obstacles on a course.

Try to position them so that the sun, and the shadows produced by the sun, present the least hazard to both horse and rider, not only at different times of the day but — for Events that run more than once during the season — at different times of the year.

5. A water complex should not appear until at least a fifth of the way into a course. Obstacles constructed in water and out of water should be both simple and straightforward. This is because the spray and the splash caused by a horse jumping into or out of water tends to obscure the obstacle, which makes it more difficult to negotiate. It is nearly impossible to measure striding in water. Different horses have different ways of going through it. Most horses trot through water, so distances beyond one stride are, generally speaking, not critical.

6. A bank, *per se*, is difficult to adapt into a challenging 'option'. However, the rails which you place before it, on it, and after it can transform a bank into an interesting complex.

It is quite possible, of course, that in an effort to outdo each other, course designers are becoming too technical and too contrived in their approach to designing not only banks but other combinations. The original Normandy Bank at Haras du Pin in France was a natural fence forming part of the existing terrain. Horses had to jump off a farm road over a ditch on to a bank and then over rails into a field below (the purpose of the rails being to keep the stock in the field). This original bank has been adapted and modified to meet special situations on courses all over the world. Some adaptations have been simplified versions, but others have been highly complex, with four or more alternative routes through them.

7. A single obstacle preceding a combination can have a great effect on how difficult the combination is to ride, depending on how close it is placed. In a similar way, single obstacles placed beyond a combination may cause more problems the closer they are related to or associated with the combination. It could take between 10 and 20 strides for a horse and rider to recover fully from jumping a significant obstacle, and it is probably safe to say that a horse could

An example of numbering and lettering. Although the successive jumping elements of this complex were at points within a stride of each other, they were numbered as separate obstacles rather than lettered, A, B, C, for three reasons: (1) If a horse refused, the rider could easily try the obstacle a second time without going back over the previous element. (2) The course designer did not want to make it possible to retake any element already jumped. (3) On a course of 32 numbered obstacles, 4 were already numbered. This obstacle was a very simple piece of construction, yet riders spent hours studying the irregular terrain and the many lines of approach, trying to decide just which route was best for their particular horse.

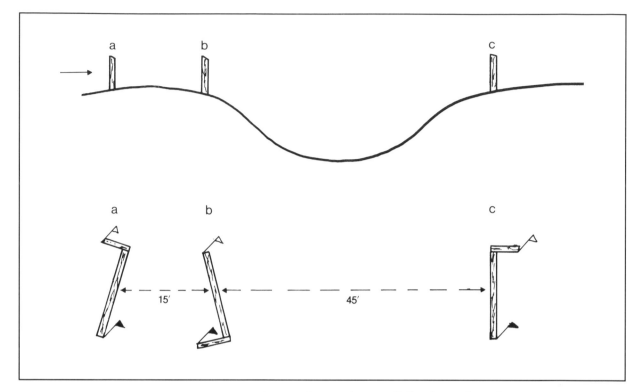

Some interesting and more difficult combinations
Chesterland: Sunken Road
The straight-through test involved a bounce into a sunken lane. The lane had sloping, not vertical sides. The first two parts were angled slightly, to give the rider a choice of distance in the bounce. All three elements had 'let out' options. The fence caused much anxiety but few penalties.

gallop up to 30 strides before the obstacle he has just negotiated will have no effect on the one he is about to tackle.

☐ Three more thoughts about striding: (a) It is far safer (and more rewarding to the bold, free-going horse) to set a 'bounce' at 15 ft or 16 ft (4.5 m to 5 m) than it is at 11 ft or 12 ft (3 m to 3.5 m), and a 'one stride' at 25 ft or 26 ft (7.5 m to 8 m) than it is at 21 ft or 22 ft (6 m to 6.5 m) though neither extreme is desirable. (b) It is unfair to a horse to place any kind of obstacle following a bullfinch, or after any kind of obstacle that requires a horse to jump 'blind', at less than three strides. (c) Under ordinary conditions, a 'bounce' on a downhill slope can be lengthened from 14 ft (4 m) to 15 ft or 16 ft (4.5 m to 5 m) and a 'bounce' on an uphill slope can be shortened from 14 ft (4 m) to 12 ft or 13 ft (3.5 m to 4 m). For some time the official recommendation has been that one-stride and two-stride distances, both on an uphill and on a downhill slope, should be similarly lengthened and shortened. As far as shortening the stride measurement on an uphill combination is concerned, this view still holds, but many people

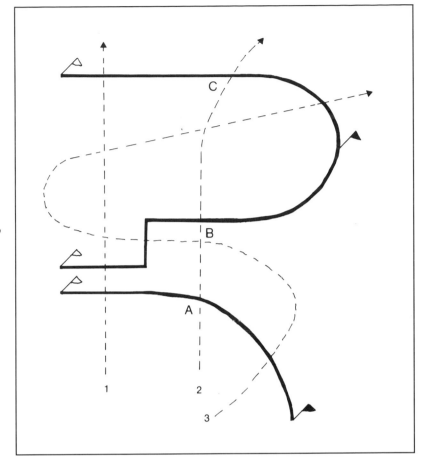

Chesterland 'S on the Hill'
Option 1. Ascending parallel with slight drop, then two strides on steep downhill slope to vertical rails.
Option 2. Bounce on downhill slope, then one short stride to vertical.
Option 3. Three separate verticals, very slow.
When first used, this combination was not a great success, as too few riders tackled options 1 or 2 — they were too difficult late in the course. Option 3 was fairly easy and riders were not prepared to risk penalties on tired horses. The slope is quite steep. A classic case of mis-judgement by the course designer.

now question whether or not all horses lengthen through downhill one-stride and two-stride combinations. They may do so on gentle slopes, but on steeper slopes they seem to check slightly and, in fact, often take shorter strides.

8. Until recent years, many course designers have incorporated in their options and combinations jumping elements that were dimensionally larger than allowed by the rules — usually on the shortest, fastest route. Now the feeling and the practice seem to be to construct all the elements of an obstacle which a horse could reasonably be expected to jump, within the limits allowed.

9. Don't be surprised if a combination copied from another course rides quite differently from the original. This can be attributed to the different terrain and site, a different series of obstacles leading up to it, different weather and footing, and possibly a different level or standard of Event.

10. Combinations that are designed at home by drafting weird and wonderful shapes on pieces of paper and then trying to find appropriate pieces of terrain on which to place them, rarely work out

165

well. A more successful way to go about it is first to decide what question or questions you want to ask of the horse and rider, then to locate which of the terrain features in the area best lends itself to this purpose (all the while keeping in mind the guidelines for positioning combinations), and finally to design the complex so that, in the most natural and unobtrusive way possible, it fits into and utilises the chosen terrain.

POINTS TO REMEMBER

A well-balanced course, particularly at the higher levels, should include combinations which test most, if not all, of the following:

(a) Boldness.
(b) Obedience.
(c) Impulsion.
(d) Holding to a given or chosen line.
(e) Balance.
(f) Turning between elements.
(g) Timing.
(h) Shortening and/or lengthening of stride between elements.

An obstacle complex should have:

(a) Well-balanced options.
(b) Clearly defined tests. If the course designer isn't sure what question he is trying to ask the horse, how can the horse or rider possibly be expected to know?
(c) Safe design. Rails where a horse could get trapped or hung up must be easily and quickly removable. Pen-type or enclosed combinations must provide an escape route. The going must be non-slip, particularly at water jumps. An all weather evacuation route is necessary, to allow access to vehicles in case of an accident.
(d) Massive construction using matching or complementary materials.
(e) Locations which provide easy viewing for spectators.
(f) An aesthetically pleasing appearance, so that the complex looks as though it belongs where it is built. Landscaping will improve the appearance of any obstacle.
(g) The use of motif, incorporating national or locally found structures, wagons, etc., which relate to the agriculture, industry, history, or architecture of the area.

DO NOT:

(a) Penalise a long-striding, bold-moving horse by making distances between elements too short. It is better to err on the long side.
(b) Ask a horse to solve a problem unless you're perfectly certain what you intend the problem to be.

(c) Place an obstacle complex at either the very beginning or the very end of a course.
(d) Waste a lot of effort designing obstacle complexes at the very lowest levels where the required speeds are slow.
(e) Punish a horse for taking the 'bold line'.
(f) Screen the horse's view of the next obstacle, or ask him to jump 'blind'.

When to Letter or Number Combinations

If the successive jumping elements of an obstacle complex are set so that should a horse refuse an element, he would find it difficult to retake it without first going back over and retaking the previous element, the complex should be lettered A,B,C, etc. If the successive elements are set so that the 'average' horse would not have to retake the previous part before re-attempting the element refused, the complex can, and probably should, be numbered 7,8,9 etc.

Two successive bounces or three banks up with a stride or less between jumping efforts would ordinarily be lettered elements of the same numbered obstacle (9A,B,C). Three successive obstacles or three banks up with, for example, three strides between jumping efforts, would ordinarily be numbered separately (7,8,9). Between these two cases the jumping elements could either be numbered or lettered. There is no definite rule to go by, and the decision will depend on common sense, safety, precedent, the (vertical and spread) dimensions of the elements — and how many lettered combinations are allowed on the course.

How many Combinations?

The FEI rules permit one lettered combination per 10 numbered obstacles. On a course of 30 numbered obstacles, 3 lettered combinations would be in order. Most Ground Juries and Technical Delegates will allow that when a course has more than an even 10 numbered obstacles, an additional lettered complex may be included. A course with from 31 to 39 numbered obstacles could therefore include 4 lettered combinations.

Most Ground Juries and Technical Delegates will also rule that an option fence such as a 'V' or corner (where the horse and rider can either go over the apex in one jump or over the two legs in two jumps) must be flagged as an A,B, but that it need not be counted as one of the lettered combinations under the 'one per ten' rule. The course designer should be ever mindful of the total number of jumping efforts he is asking the horse to make and should keep to a minimum this type of obstacle — perhaps one or two at the most.

Recommended Distances

A very experienced course designer will know how to adapt distances between the elements of combinations according to the type of fence, the terrain, and the standard of horse and rider. However, on *flat ground* the following will ride well for most horses.

In general terms, the lower the obstacles, the shorter the distance between them should be. Unlike those in show jumping, cross-country fences are never so high that they cause a horse to land closer to a fence.

Vertical to Vertical

Bounce	13'6"–15'	(4.00 m–4.50 m)
1 Stride	24'–27'	(7.30 m–8.20 m)
2 Strides	35'–38'	(10.50 m–11.50 m)

Vertical to Parallel (Oxer)
or
Parallel (Oxer) to Vertical

Bounce	12'–14'	(3.60 m–4.20 m)
1 Stride	24'–26'	(7.30 m–7.90 m)
2 Strides	35'–36'	(10.50 m–11.50 m)

Parallel (Oxer) to Parallel

Bounce	not recommended	
1 Stride	24'–25'	(7.30 m–7.50 m)
2 Strides	35'–36'	(10.50 m–10.90 m)

On gentle downhill slopes the horse will naturally lengthen his stride; on all uphill slopes he will shorten it.
On steep downhill slopes he will shorten his stride.

Steps — Up and Down:

(Bounce)	9'	(2.70 m)

Bank (Normandy Type):

(Bounce)	10'6"–11'	(3.20m–3.30m)

Flat or Round Topped Bank:
(Bounce)	12'–13'	(3.60 m–3.90 m)
1 Stride	21'–24'	(6.40 m–7.20 m)

Rails to Step Up
(not a comfortable fence to ride)
Bounce	12'–13'	(3.60 m–3.90 m)
1 Stride	23'–24'	(7.00 m–7.20 m)

Rails to Step Down
Bounce	10'–11'	(3.00 m–3.30 m)
1 Stride	20'–21'	(6.00 m–6.40 m)

Step up to Rails
Bounce	9'	(2.70 m)
1 Stride	18'–20'	(5.40 m–6.00 m)

Step down to Rails
Bounce	12'	(3.60 m)
1 Stride	21'	(6.40 m)

These distances are only intended to be a guideline. They will be appropriate at all levels for relatively straightforward fences.

At the highest levels of competition, where combinations may be sited on unusual terrain, only the most experienced course designer can set the distances.

Coffins:

Rails/Ditch/Rails: 1 Stride — Normal 18'–20' (5.40 m–6.00 m)
                   1 Stride — Medium 15' (4.50 m)
only suitable on steep slopes and at very high levels where the most experienced course designer can set the distances.

Ditch to Rails:	Bounce	12'	(3.60 m)
	1 Stride	18'–20'	(5.40–6.00 m)

All distances are measured *inside to inside* of the fences, except in the case of a *corner* (or V) in a combination, which should be measured from the middle of the spread, i.e. a line bisecting the corner.

All Distances over Two Strides
In principle add 11′–13′ (3.30 m–3.90 m) per stride.
As distances get longer they also become less critical, as there is scope for horse and rider to adjust their stride.

If the course designer is uncertain as to what the distance between two elements of a complex should be, he may decide either (a) to set the two elements at a slight angle to each other, or (b) to design one of the elements in the shape of a crescent, so that varying distances are offered to the competitor. For example, an 'in and out' designed as a bounce could be set (assuming that the frontage is at least 24 ft/7.20 m) with a distance of 11 ft 6 in/3.50 m at the left extremity, and 18 ft/5.40 m at the right extremity. This leaves the choice to the rider, and lets the course designer 'off the hook'.

Competition Organisation and Control

(a) Checking the Cross-Country Course and Fences

You must ensure that clear, accurate plans of the course are provided: preferably in the programme, at the Start, and at the Secretary's tent or office. Before any affiliated Horse Trial can take place, an official course inspection is held. For major International Three-Day Events the FEI will appoint a Technical Delegate to approve the course. For all standard Three-Day Events the Ground Jury will have this final responsibility. For other Events, a steward or some other official will be appointed, to make sure that the dimensions of the obstacles and the administrative arrangements are acceptable.

The course designer must aim to have everything ready at least 24 hours before the course inspection. Last-minute problems always arise, and with so little time left to deal with them it is vital not to be building or altering fences during this period.

The designer's main task during the final few days before a competition is to tidy up the fences and to make sure that they look as attractive as possible.

Try to look at the fences as though you were seeing them for the first time, and think how they can be made to look as inviting to the horse and as attractive to the spectator as possible.

(b) Communications

Though others may be responsible for the actual work involved, a course designer must concern himself with every single aspect of the cross-country phase of an Event. The positioning of the cross-country Control Centre, and its efficiency, are perhaps the most important factors. Good communications are essential for efficient scoring and commentary. Above all, they are vital for the safety of competitors — by means of effective liaison with emergency services such as doctor, ambulance, vet or fence repair party.

(c) The Start and Finish Area

You will be responsible for the layout and supervision of the Start and Finish area. This includes the position of the warm-up or

Left, above: *Measuring the spread at the top of the fence.*

Left, below: *Measuring the base of the spread.*

Right: *The Start Box.*

practice fences (flagged), the run-in from the Finish, which must be safe, the Weighing Tent (if applicable) and any other necessary tent, caravan, or trailer which may be used by officials.

Important: Remember that Timekeepers *must* have clear lines of vision. This can be critical to the results of the competition.

Layout: Start and Finish. First fence and last fence.

(d) Flags and other Markers

The course itself must be marked with red (right) and white (left) boundary flags, to define obstacles and the Start and Finish. Direction arrows, fence numbers and, if there is more than one class, appropriate indicators, are also required. The most effective way to distinguish between the obstacles to be jumped in each class is to use different colours for the indicators and fence numbers. Unless the marking system is specified in the official rules, you must devise your own method of indicating the different courses as clearly as possible.

The course designer should supervise the flagging of obstacles. Sometimes the difficulty of a fence can be altered dramatically by the exact position of the flag — for example, on a corner fence — and if the obstacles have been designed to have a certain degree of difficulty you should make sure that the flags are put in exactly the right place.

There are no specific rules applying to the shape and size of flags, arrows, numbers, or other markers — but remember that whatever you use they should be clear and conspicuous.

Flags must be fixed securely to a fence so that they cannot be easily dislodged. They should not be attached by anything which could cause injury should a horse accidentally run into them, nor should a flag be nailed on to an obstacle in any place where a horse could jump over it.

If it is necessary to provide 'compulsory' flags to make competitors cover the correct distance or to avoid a hazardous piece of

Numbering a fence.

Flagging a fence.

A numbered and flagged fence.

Roping

A. A straightforward fence in direct line.

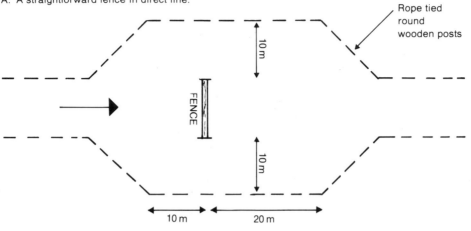

Rope tied
round
wooden posts

FENCE

10 m

10 m

10 m

20 m

B. A fence on a turn (allow enough space to approach)

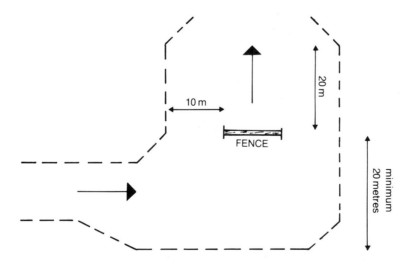

10 m

20 m

FENCE

minimum
20 metres

NB All rope must be tied on wooden stakes,
so that if a horse goes into it the rope will come off.

ground, they must be large and conspicuous. Both red and white flags should be used. Set them wide apart to allow a smooth turn and to avoid poaching the ground. Make sure that all flags, including compulsory ones, as well as the route and obstacle numbers, are shown clearly on the course maps.

(e) Roping

The amount of roping required on a course will depend entirely on the size of the crowds expected. If in doubt, it is sensible to provide too much roping rather than too little; it is not there to help competitors find their way, but to ensure safety.

Areas which particularly need protection, no matter how small the Event, are the Start and Finish; also any 'blind spots' such as the landing side of fences set in hedgerows where spectators cannot see competitors approaching, or where hills and slopes may also obscure vision.

The course designer should assume that there will always be somebody walking about an Event who is nearly blind or totally deaf and unaware that a horse is approaching at the gallop, and should rope the course accordingly.

If extensive roping is required, the designer must consider appropriate places where spectators may cross the course, and must mark such crossing points clearly so that they can see where to go. When an entire cross-country course, or large areas of it, are being roped, a track of 11 yd (10 m) should be ample. Where horses are only galloping, 5 yd (4·5 m) are generally wide enough.

If large numbers of spectators are expected, the roping at obstacles should be arranged to provide the best possible view from both sides. (See diagram on page 176.)

At major Events it will be necessary to provide more robust fencing than rope or string around obstacles where crowds are likely to congregate. Chestnut paling — though not easy to erect — is an ideal barrier for this purpose. Snow fencing (e.g. strong nylon mesh) is one of the best alternatives. A narrow walkway within the paling can be roped off, for use by senior officials and accredited press representatives. In a Three-Day Event, or at some One-Day Horse Trials, the penalty zones must be effectively roped off so that spectators do not stray into them.

(f) Spectators

It is very easy to underestimate the effect which spectators have on horses. A horse will usually concentrate on the track and the obstacles in front of him, but if these are not adequately roped or fenced off there may be occasions when he is ostensibly being asked to jump into a solid bank of people. This will make horses nervous, and therefore the fence will jump badly. Always ensure that the horse can clearly see the area where he will be landing and, preferably, a track leading away from the fence, and that he is not asked to head straight for a wall of spectators.

When roping a course (as when planning its layout) make sure that emergency vehicles will be able to move around without difficulty. During bad weather it has been known for Events to be cancelled not because ground conditions have made the fences unjumpable, but because emergency vehicles (e.g. ambulances) would not have been able to get to an obstacle. Suitable routes should be discussed in detail with the official vet, doctor, and ambulance service; and all those concerned during an Event should be thoroughly briefed.

Fence judges must also be able to reach their positions, and, again, the best route for them to take should be considered in advance. The course designer, with perhaps the Technical Delegate or official Steward, should check that the judges are positioned satisfactorily and safely. At some complex obstacles the fence judge may need an assistant.

(g) Penalty Zones

According to FEI rules 'The penalty zone is an area in which a horse and rider will be penalized for a fall, circle, refusal or run-out. It must not restrict the horse's room to manoeuvre as he negotiates the obstacle. If, in exceptional circumstances, it does so restrict, then the Technical Delegate or the Ground Jury have the right to extend it.'

A course designer of any Three-Day Event or of a One-Day Horse Trial where penalty zones are used will find the marking out very time consuming. While International Rules on penalty zones may seem clear, the interpretation of them differs considerably. It is important to be absolutely consistent over the entire course. A zone must be very clearly marked, for the benefit of the competitors and the fence judge.

In making a penalty zone, the course designer must err on the side of generosity to the rider, which means that where there are several alternative routes at a fence he must allow a full zone for each route. This particularly applies at combinations. For example: there must be 21 yd (20 m) on the landing side of all the possible routes through an obstacle.

The limits of a penalty zone must be marked at the corners with pegs or flags. The perimeters of the zone must also be clearly defined on the ground itself. This is particularly important at combination fences, or at fences where competitors are likely to incur penalties. Unless the boundary is clearly marked it will be impossible for a fence judge to decide whether a horse has crossed the line of a penalty zone or whether a rider has fallen inside or outside the zone. If the grass is long enough, the most practical way of achieving this is to mow a line which will remain visible throughout the day and in any weather. Other methods are with whitewash or sawdust, but these will be less satisfactory in wet or muddy conditions.

(h) On-Course Repairs and Adjustments

Finally, you must be prepared for adjusting and/or repairing fences on the day of the Event, either because they have been damaged, or because the going has deteriorated, or simply because they have to be used in different ways for different classes. In the latter case they must obviously be built in such a way that they can readily be altered.

It is essential to have an efficient team of helpers for carrying out swift repairs. You should also have a stock pile of spare timber, and other essential materials (such as rope, staples, wire, hand tools) placed at strategic positions around the course; if it all has to be carted on a slow tractor from a central position, a lot of time will be wasted. The ideal vehicle for a repair party is a Land-Rover or similar four-wheel drive vehicle with a small trailer.

Usually during a competition only minor running repairs are necessary. A broken rail can be replaced easily if the obstacle was constructed with this eventuality in mind. The worst type of problem is a post which has broken off or shifted considerably in the ground, and the most satisfactory way of dealing with this potentially disastrous situation is to fix struts to the fence, rather than putting in new posts in the very short time available.

Having given due attention to the obstacles, the course designer must consider the going, and be ready to deal with places where it might deteriorate unexpectedly. For this you must have ready a supply of small grade stones, sand, or ash.

Communications and Control System

This book applies to that part of an Event organisation concerned with the cross-country and show jumping courses. The control system plays a vital part in these aspects of the competition, and the course designer must be involved in their planning. On the cross-country, every fence must be accessible to a vehicle for the possible evacuation of an injured horse or rider, and the routes that these emergency vehicles may take to get to and from the obstacles must be planned in advance. The designers/builders concerned with the dressage and show jumping arenas should also be conversant with — and consulted about — the control system.

Communications will often depend on the budget, but there are certain essentials. Every fence judge or steward must be able to contact personnel at Control HQ to inform them of any accident or problem. This is best achieved with a telephone or a radio at every fence, but in many cases it will only be possible to provide radios at strategic points around the course where several obstacles can be seen. The fence-judges will then be able to communicate with each of these 'Outposts' by waving coloured flags to indicate that they need the doctor, fence repair party or veterinary surgeon.

Control HQ must be in a position to communicate with the fence judges or with appointed helpers at strategic points in the course, so that instructions can be given for the stopping of horses if there should be an accident. Under FEI Rules it is now recommended that there should be at least two official 'stopping points' on the course.

Positioning of Jump Judge

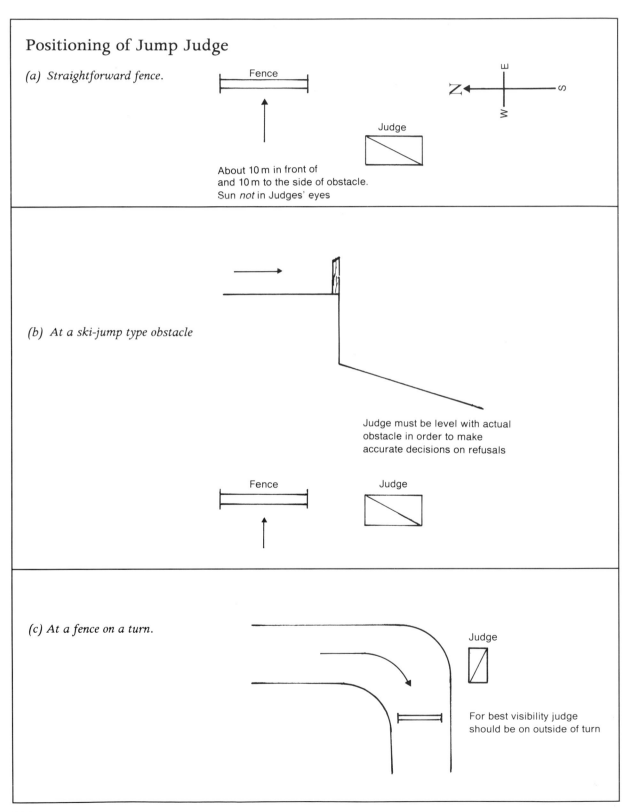

(a) Straightforward fence.

Fence

Judge

About 10 m in front of
and 10 m to the side of obstacle.
Sun *not* in Judges' eyes

(b) At a ski-jump type obstacle

Judge must be level with actual
obstacle in order to make
accurate decisions on refusals

Fence

Judge

(c) At a fence on a turn.

Judge

For best visibility judge
should be on outside of turn

They should be sited at least 50 metres away from an obstacle, and competitors should be shown them when they walk the course.

The stopping points must be clearly marked on the course with coloured posts or other prominent indicators. It is strongly re-commended that at all Three-Day Events stopping pegs should be provided at the approach to every obstacle, as far away from that obstacle as the fence judge can reasonably see accurately, so that *wherever* a horse may have to be stopped on the course there is always a reference point at which his time can be taken. This is particularly useful when riders of different nationalities are compet-ing; because of language difficulties they may not be able to confer with the fence judge in order to find out where they are to re-start.

Control HQ should have absolute command of the cross-country course throughout the running of the competition and must have direct contact with the doctor, vet and fence repair party. All of these should have a radio, but wherever possible representatives of each emergency service should be actually located at Control and should be despatched from there to any incident. Control will also have to be in touch with the central organisation: i.e. the Secretary's Office, the Official Steward, the Technical Delegate and/or the Ground Jury, depending on who is in charge on the day of the competition.

Efficient communication between Control and the start of the cross-country phase is vital. It will enable Control to 'Hold the Start' when there is an incident on the course, thus avoiding a bottle-neck of competitors stopped during their round.

A well-organised communications system will not only control the competition and make it as safe as possible for the competitors. It will also provide information for the commentators and the public address system. Ideally, Control and commentators should be aware of any penalties incurred by horses at each obstacle, and should know from the Start/Finish the time taken by every horse on the course. The commentator should be able to broadcast a provisional score for a horse soon after he goes through the Finish, thus contributing immeasurably to the interest of competitors and spectators alike. An efficient system will also ensure that any doubtful penalties can be investigated very quickly. If, for example, it is announced that a rider has had a refusal and he wishes to lodge an objection he may thus do so immediately, without waiting to see the scores go up on the board.

The exact siting of loudspeakers for the public address is a highly technical matter which the contractor should deal with. However, the course designer must ensure that the speakers are not positioned in any inappropriate places, too close to an obstacle for instance, which would deafen or distract either people or horses. He must also ensure that wires are always laid safely, away from the course, and out of the reach of spectators.

Three-Day Events

THE ROADS AND TRACKS

Roads and Tracks make up the first and third phases (A and C) of the Speed and Endurance Test in a Two-Day or Three-Day Event.

Careful planning is necessary to determine which routes to use and what distance to cover. Rough ground, for example, can add to the severity and can affect the competitors' enjoyment of the Event. Recommended distances for Roads and Tracks can be found in the rules of the FEI or in those of the national governing body, as appropriate. If circumstances allow, you should try to make Phase C approximately twice as long as Phase A. A very long Phase A achieves nothing. On the other hand, it must be long enough (at least $1\frac{3}{4}$ miles or 3 kilometres) to serve its purpose, which is to warm up the horse for the Steeplechase course.

The location of the Steeplechase will have the greatest influence on the length and route of the Roads and Tracks, and is far more important than the precise distances of A and C. Ideally, the start point of Phase A should be near the stables and/or lorry park. This phase will take horses to the start of the Steeplechase, which for the convenience of spectators should be sited not far from the cross-country. Phase C will then be over a longer route, to allow the horses to recover from the exertion of the Steeplechase, and to complete the remaining distance without undue stress. They will finish up at the Box for a ten-minute compulsory halt before the start of Phase D.

Initially the Roads and Tracks can be measured out to scale, with a piece of string and a good map. You can follow up by driving round the actual course in a vehicle which has an accurate speedometer. The designer must ensure that the distance, time allowed/optimum time, time limit, etc, for each class is correct and that the route is clearly signed with kilometre markers and direction indicators.

Several types of going and terrain can be suitable for Roads and Tracks. It is not necessary for them to be run over beautiful parkland turf; footing can vary from hard tarmac roads and paths to grass or woodland rides. However, although the going on the Roads and Tracks is not nearly as important as it is on the other phases of a Three-Day Event (as the horses are moving slowly), it is important to avoid very rough or deep or wet ground, which could cause injury.

The speed required on the Roads and Tracks at all levels of competition is 220 m (240 yd) per minute, which is about 12.75 kilometres (8½ miles) per hour. To achieve this, horses have to go at a steady trot, though some riders will prefer to walk part of the way and to canter part of the way. On Phase A all riders will wish to have a sharp canter at some stage in order to ensure that their horse is adequately warmed up for the Steeplechase.

If it is possible to drive around the Roads and Tracks, it will make it easier to show this part of the course to the competitors. During the competition, also, the chief Roads and Tracks steward may have to go round in his vehicle from time to time. This does not mean that every metre must be accessible to motor traffic, but stretches of road and track that can only be negotiated on foot or on a horse should be kept to the absolute minimum.

The whole competition will be much more manageable if the start point of Phase A is located away from the cross-country Box, ideally very close to the stables or lorry park, and not in the same area as the finish of C and start of D.

Methods of marking the Roads and Tracks vary around the world. The critical factor is to ensure that all competitors can easily find their way around; it is not intended as a memory test. The rules specify that clear markers should be put up at each completed kilometre from the start of each phase. They will be marked *1 km A*, for example, or *2 kms C*. Arrows or discs must be used to indicate a change in direction or a slight deviation, or to confirm the route where necessary. After an intersection, a fork in the road, or a sharp turn, it is helpful to place an 'A' or a 'C', as the case may be, to reassure the competitor that he has gone the correct way and is on course. The markers which show up best are black letters ('A' or 'C') on yellow panels 8 in × 18 in, preferably in phosphorescent paint. It is also helpful to place an 'A' or 'C' beacon at least every 200–300 m. When there is no possibility of confusion, blank markers will suffice.

Finally, check-points will be needed on each phase of Roads and Tracks, for which you will have to provide extra officials. From the administrative point of view, and to avoid unfortunate error, the course designer should try to reduce these to the minimum. However, the object of a check-point is to ensure that there are no major short cuts allowing competitors to cut off substantial parts of the course. Each point must have both red and white flags.

THE CROSS-COUNTRY BOX

The Cross-country Box is used only in Three-Day Events, or in Two-Day Events where Roads and Tracks are included in the Speed and Endurance phase. It is sited at the end of the second Roads and Tracks (Phase C), the area in which horses arrive before proceeding to the cross-country. An absolute minimum size for the Box should

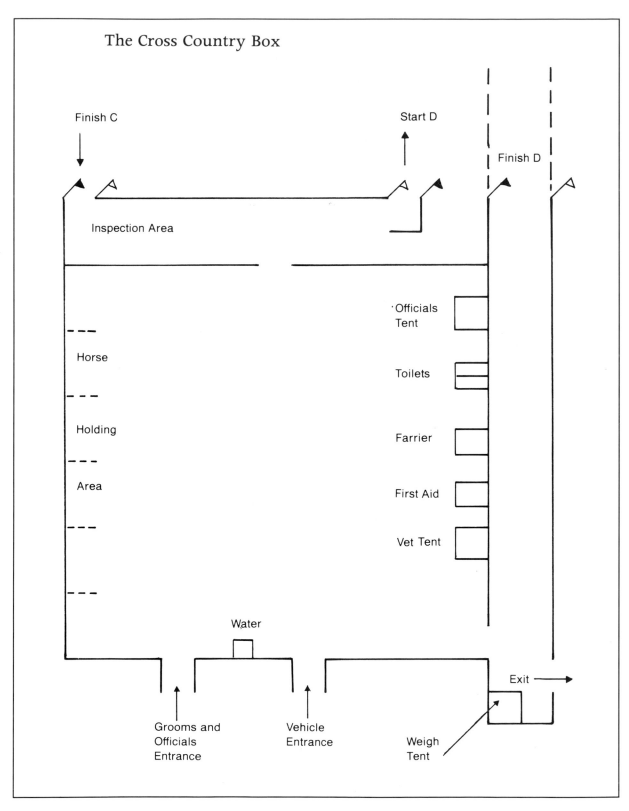

The Cross Country Box

Finish C

Start D

Finish D

Inspection Area

Officials Tent

Horse

Toilets

Holding

Farrier

Area

First Aid

Vet Tent

Water

Exit

Grooms and Officials Entrance

Vehicle Entrance

Weigh Tent

be 30 m × 20 m (33 yd × 22yd), but even double that would not be too large.

The main purpose of the Box is to provide an area where competitors can be administered to during the compulsory ten-minute half, and where an official inspection can take place to ensure that a horse is fit enough to continue on Phase D. The two laymen and one vet who carry out this inspection must have adequate facilities in which to do a quick and professional job. As so much activity takes place in the Box it is much better to have too much space than too little. A suitable layout can be seen on page 184. It shows that there should be plenty of room to make a first check on horses as soon as they arrive from Phase C. Equally important, the horses could be brought back here before starting Phase D some ten minutes later, so that where a Panel has been in some doubt about fitness, they will be able to see the horse again before it is due to go on the final cross-country phase.

As well as allowing for several horses to be in at any one time, with their riders and grooms, enough space must also be provided for the farrier, vet, water points, toilets, and any other necessary services. Also, several officials have to work within the Box — including the stewards responsible for getting horses to the start of Phase D on time. All of them need room for manoeuvre. The Box should, if possible, be surrounded by fairly robust fencing. Ideally there should be a steward at the entrance to prevent non-participating members of the public from entering.

One of the factors most often forgotten in the initial planning stage is that the Start and the Finish of the cross-country will be next to each other, and very close to the Box. After the finish of Phase D, competitors need a run-in of at least 100 m (109 yd). For a major competition there should also be a weighing-in area. After weighing-in, the competitors should not have to return through the Box area in order to take their horses back to the stables.

10-Minute Halt Box

1. There must be a suitable area, clear of horses and officials, for the Inspection Panel to check horses as they finish Phase 'D'.
2. Ideally the Finish 'D' and Weigh Scales should be outside the main part of the Box, so that horses which have finished do not interfere with those on the 10-minute halt.
3. The Start of Phase 'A' should definitely be separated from the main Box.
4. There should be a narrow, manned, pedestrian entrance and a vehicle entrance to allow a horse or human ambulance to drive into the Box.
5. The Weigh Scales must be at least 50 metres and preferably up to 100 metres after the Finish of 'D'.
6. In hot weather, shade in the Box is invaluable. This can best be provided by trees!
7. The exact layout will depend above all on the direction of the Start and Finish 'D' and Finish 'C'. The diagram shows one possibility.

THE STEEPLECHASE

In laying out a Steeplechase course the most important factor is the going. Consistency is critical, and variations are not acceptable. This means that the entire course must be on one type of ground. Although sand or dirt are adequate — as long as they are carefully harrowed and neither too deep nor too hard — well-tended turf in good condition will produce the best surface.

It is perfectly acceptable to include some slopes, but not really steep hills. If there are gentle slopes, the positioning of the fences, and particularly the planning of the bends and corners, will be absolutely vital. Each situation is likely to vary, so it is impossible to specify exactly what radius a bend should have. As a guide, however, a course which is less than 1 kilometre in circumference will almost certainly have bends that are too tight.

In this phase, horses will be going at a strong gallop. At the top level of international competition the speed required is 690 metres per minute, which is about the same speed as a fairly slow race over fences. For Juniors under International Rules this speed comes down to 640 metres per minute. The various National Rules may specify other speeds, which will be within this range.

Steeplechase open ditch with number, flag and wing.

The course can be circular, oval, or shaped like a figure-of-eight or similar figure. When deciding on a design, the conclusive argument must always be the suitability of the terrain for a particular configuration. As it is unnecessary to have the start and finish of the Steeplechase in the same place, the ground can be used to the best advantage without having to worry about the horses finishing where they started.

The roping and fencing on a Steeplechase course is important. It may be essential to rope the whole of the inside track. When few spectators are expected, and the layout is obvious, only the bends need roping, but if in doubt use more roping rather than less.

The fences on the Steeplechase must be flagged and numbered in the usual way. It is advisable to avoid the use of turning flags, but it will still be necessary to flag the bends. The flags must be distinct and clearly visible. To emphasise their position they can be attached to a strong hurdle or similar object.

Though types of obstacle may vary from country to country, there are some basic principles which should be observed. The maximum height permitted under International Rules is 1.4 m or 4 ft 7 in, but in practice this often seems too big; approximately 1.3 m (4 ft 3 in) is a more suitable size. However, more Steeplechase courses tend to have obstacles which are too small, so that horses jump them badly, rather than too large.

As the Steeplechase is not intended as a test of jumping ability, the fences must be constructed so that a horse is encouraged to jump them at a strong gallop without having to check or adjust his stride unduly. This means that they must be substantial, sloping, and with clearly defined take-off boards and high wings, in order to invite consistent and bold jumping.

Four metres should be regarded as a minimum width for a steeplechase fence; the best ones are wider than this: up to 6–7 metres (6½–7½ yds). The fences should always have high, robust wings, and care should be taken to ensure that the wings will be safe should an uncontrolled horse crash through them.

The fixed part of a Steeplechase fence — i.e. the timber framing — must not exceed 1 m (3 ft 3 in) in height, and the poles should be clearly visible on the front of the fence so that the horse knows exactly where the solid part of the jump ends and where the soft brush begins. A slope of about 60° on the face of the fence will provide the most inviting profile for a horse to jump. The wings should be at least 2 m (6 ft 6 in) and preferably 3 m (9 ft 10 in) wide and should be set at an angle to the fence, thus helping to draw the horse into the obstacle. This is shown on the line drawing on page 69.

In Great Britain, Three-Day Events generally have Steeplechase fences which closely resemble the obstacles used for National Hunt racing. These can be constructed anywhere in the world, with timber frames and brush or birch in-filling, as on page 119. However, perfectly satisfactory obstacles can be made with an internal base of straw bales and only a covering of birch. At

Luhmühlen, one of the most attractive courses, many of the obstacles on the Steeplechase are natural hedges grown on low banks, walls, etc.

The only consistent requisite for Steeplechase fences must be that a galloping horse can brush through the top of them. Solid, fixed fences should not be acceptable. In the past, some courses included rails set 1 metre (3 ft 3 in) high but they achieved little, and interfered with the flowing gallop rhythm intended in this phase.

The Rider's View of the Cross-Country Course

Why Walk the Course?

Whether riding in a competition or practising over cross-country fences, however simple, *always* study the course of obstacles carefully before jumping it, to plan exactly where to go and how to tackle each fence, and to avoid making uncomfortable and unnecessary mistakes.

Never assume that the fences you will be jumping are safe, with sound take-offs and landings. Ground conditions can alter unexpectedly overnight — after heavy rain for example — or fresh rabbit holes or a new wire fence or piece of machinery may suddenly appear on the landing side.

When schooling, you may either walk or ride up to the fences, to examine each one and decide on your line of approach and the best place to jump. Before a competition, however, this has to be done on foot.

How a rider approaches and jumps each obstacle will depend on the type and difficulty of the fence itself, the ground around it (the going, undulations), and the positions of both the previous fence and one which follows. For the more experienced competitor, when speed becomes an important factor, shortcuts and angles may also need consideration. Some riders have a natural 'eye' for cross-country riding, assessing at a glance the ideal approach to an obstacle, and knowing by instinct the best place to jump it. Others may have to work much harder to acquire this ability.

At the highest levels, walking a course becomes a skill which, although based on common sense, requires a thorough knowledge of horses, as well as the experience which results from both study and practice. When faced with a greater variety of obstacles, such as intricate combinations, optional routes and 'problem' fences, the courage and jumping ability of the horse are not enough, and accuracy and precision on the part of the rider become increasingly important. This means not only improving riding skills and the horse's schooling, but also learning how to assess a course as a whole and to study each obstacle with detailed attention.

Whatever the level of competition, the rider must walk the course with the aim of choosing a track best suited to the particular horse. A novice rider or anyone riding an inexperienced horse should aim for a safe, clear round, which often means taking the easiest, not the quickest, ways. Both horse and rider are then likely to enjoy the experience and should thus gain in confidence.

It is unwise to enter a competition unless you are certain that both you and your horse are well up to the standard that the course demands. The lowest levels of cross-country are not necessarily the easiest. Where possible, choose well-designed and solidly-built courses on good ground, which the horse will jump better than a sub-standard course. One ill-conceived fence could put him off badly.

As the obstacles become more demanding, the rider's skill at approaching them correctly and with the right amount of speed and impulsion becomes more important. A successful ride round the course will depend more than ever on how well you have studied it on foot. Too often we see the courage, athletic ability and experience of a horse abused, particularly when ridden too fast and inaccurately.

Walking the Course

Before you set out to walk, look at a map of the course. You will then see the general direction and the length, and you will notice any special features. If a programme is provided, this may include a description of each fence as well as a map showing the route, so take it with you. You can then check that you have not missed any obstacle, alternative route, or turning-flag, as you walk the course. Any such error would incur elimination.

If there is more than one class and the courses differ in any way, you need to know which coloured fence numbers and direction markers to follow for your particular class. The obstacles will have red flags or markers on the right-hand side, white on the left. The same colours are used for turning-flags.

During a One-Day Event there may not be time to walk the course more than once. However, an inexperienced rider should plan to get there early enough to walk it thoroughly at least twice — first to gain an overall impression of the terrain, the obstacles, and the direction to take; and then again, preferably in the company of an expert, to study each fence in detail and to work out any problems. At the top end of the scale some riders may walk at least three times round a Three-Day or a difficult One-Day Event course.

Though it may be more fun to walk the course in a group, the advantages of exchanging ideas and opinion can be outweighed by the distraction of chatter between fences. You should not be over-influenced by what fellow competitors intend to do. Listen to all points of view, but the final decision must be yours, with your own horse in mind. Many competitors prefer to go on their final walk alone, concentrating on taking the exact route which they intend to ride, and visualising the whole course clearly in their mind.

For a One-Day Event, the cross-country course is seldom roped off, so you must mentally rope it off for yourself as you walk round. Even if the route *is* confined by roping or fencing, there will still be a quickest or best way to ride it, to avoid wasting ground and to plan a quick getaway on the landing side of each obstacle.

Where ground conditions are generally good, make a habit of walking the direct route between fences. You can then assess how to be quicker than anyone who may be going perhaps faster but further. On hilly ground, if the shortest way involves climbing straight up a steep slope and down again, you should plan to skirt the hill. This will take less out of your horse and could also be quicker.

Choose where you may let the horse gallop on faster between fences without losing control. A flat or upward-sloping grassy track or field is ideal, but do not gallop fast downhill until your horse is perfectly balanced.

Make it as easy as possible for your horse by choosing the best ground, both between fences and in the approach itself. Always plan to go as straight as the terrain permits, since a bending route can unbalance a horse and interfere with his rhythm and concentration. It is important, however, to avoid rough, bumpy footing or soft, boggy patches which could deteriorate further during the competition. Look out for hazards, such as blind or ill-defined ditches, tree roots, logs, or deep ruts, which could cause a stumble, or even risk injury or a fall.

Studying the Fences

Assess each obstacle carefully so that you can see where the problems lie. Even the smallest one can cause trouble if awkwardly sited.

Try to look at each fence from the horse's viewpoint: where would *he* best like to jump it? Horses invariably jump solid-looking fences better than flimsy ones. A strongly constructed obstacle may seem formidable to the rider, but if it is clearly defined to the horse he is able to assess it early and judge it more easily.

Always aim to ride straight at the centre of a fence, unless there is a good reason for doing otherwise, such as a more attractive take-off or landing to one side, or a lower, easier place to jump. Sometimes it will be safe to jump a straightforward fence at an angle to save time, but you must be careful not to make the angle too acute and risk a run-out, or make the fence much wider and more difficult than necessary.

Generally, large spread fences and soft brush type obstacles may be tackled at a strong pace, but more precision and control will be necessary to negotiate upright or downhill fences. Those which involve an angle or turns, water, or a combination of obstacles, need particularly careful planning by the rider.

Beware of a false groundline (see page 32) which makes a fence deceptive to your horse. It will need accurate riding. Shadows can

also cause optical illusions, and it is a good idea to walk the course at the approximate time that you will be jumping it during the competition. You will then see the effects of the sun on a particular fence, and where the shadows are likely to be. This applies particularly when jumping from the light into the darkness of a wood.

Some obstacles *invite* refusals. A horse is naturally suspicious of jumping into the unknown when he cannot see where to land. Walk drop fences with this in mind, aiming to give your horse time to assess the obstacle ahead, while deciding how fast to approach it and exactly where to increase the pace.

Coffin-type obstacles should also be studied carefully. Even a very small rail as the first element can stop a horse if he suddenly sees that the ground 'disappears' on the landing side, down to a ditch, or water, or other obstacle. Always plan to approach slowly, with controlled impulsion. The horse then has time to see the ditch, recover from the surprise, and still be able to jump it.

The same principle certainly applies to water obstacles. Water is often a 'stopper' because a horse cannot know how deep it is, or how firm is its base. It should not be ridden fast, especially if it is more than 6 in (15 cm deep.) Generally, you should aim to approach it at a trot or collected canter, slightly increasing the impulsion and length of stride before take-off, to encourage a flattish trajectory. If the horse jumps too big and round into water, he will land too steeply, and may peck or even fall.

Wade through any water obstacle to test the depth and to feel how sound and level the bottom is. Remember that most surfaces will eventually deteriorate if all the horses are landing in about the same spot. If you are riding late in the order it may be wiser to choose a route slightly to one side to avoid a 'trough' or muddier patch.

At a Three-Day Event

There is plenty of time during a Three-Day Event to walk the course as often as you like, until you know it thoroughly.

Before you set off to inspect the *Roads and Tracks*, Phases A and C (in vehicles) there will be a competitors' briefing, pointing out special rules and features. Try to get a good view of the route; if you are sitting in the back or peering sideways through a window, a second look will be necessary. You have to take note of each kilometre marker and any compulsory flags or turning points. Some riders like to have a short, sharp sprint during Phase A, to clear the horse's wind before the Steeplechase, Phase B, but a suitable stretch of good ground is not always available to do this, and a strong uphill trot may have to suffice instead. Decide where best to trot or canter, aiming to arrive as fresh as possible at the start of Phase B, and with at least two minutes to spare, to alter your stirrups, check the girths and your stop-watch.

Walk the *Steeplechase* carefully, and don't forget that it will look different at the gallop. In particular, notice how tight the turns are,

Approaching water. Seen from the landing side, this obstacle asks a horse to jump boldly but neatly on to a steep bank before entering the river. He is not likely to see the water until he is about to take off, so the rider must be prepared to give extra support and confidence.

193

and look out for any confusing ropes. There are usually about 10 sloping obstacles. It is important to go the shortest way but if, 'on the day', conditions are wet and the inside track becomes cut up or slippery, be prepared to go slightly wider.

On a flat course, aim to ride at an even speed, but if it is undulating or includes some tight turns this will affect how fast you plan to go over particular sections of the course.

Work out the half-way point on the course so that you will be able to check your speed during the competition. Some riders like to note third or quarter points, too.

The amount of time that your horse takes to recover from his exertions on the Steeplechase Phase will affect your timing on Phase C, and how you ride it. If you intend to walk for most of the first kilometre, until the horse stops blowing, you must then decide on the best ground further on where you may canter to make up the lost time.

Plan to arrive in the Box, for the compulsory ten-minute halt, with at least two extra minutes to spare.

For Phase D, the *Cross-Country*, the course is likely to be roped, which will limit your choice of route. Remember that on the day crowds of people will be surrounding the fences, and try to imagine how it will look to your horse. Penalty zones (see p. 178) will be marked out around each obstacle. Study these, particularly at combination fences, where the zones may overlap, and make sure that you understand where you may or may not go — or fall off — without incurring penalties.

Finally, be prepared for your horse to feel tired towards the end. You may have to take, where possible, the easiest, least demanding options instead of the route you originally intended. The judgement of pace throughout the phases of a Three-Day Event largely depends on common sense and knowing your horse. It is obviously better to have a little surplus energy left at the end than an exhausted horse: the experience should be enjoyable for *both* of you.

194

Part 2
DRESSAGE

The Dressage
Arena

The dressage phase of a Horse Trial can have as much influence on the final result as can the cross-country. Since each of the good marks awarded by the judge is hard earned and can prove decisive, it is only fair that conditions should be as close to the ideal as possible for both competitors and judges.

THE SITE

☐ Dressage arenas should be sited on well-drained land.

Completely flat ground can be difficult to find, but a slight slope is more acceptable than a rough or uneven surface which would affect the performance of even the best moving or best trained horse.

☐ Suitable going is crucial to a good dressage test.

Wet, deep, rough or patchy ground can upset the rhythm and balance of the horse, and often his confidence, too. Also, if the going deteriorates during a competition, early starters will have an unfair advantage.

Very hard ground, which jars the feet, is unsuitable and unpopular. It discourages freedom of movement and can cause lameness. Another disadvantage of this type of going is that it can become worse after a large number of horses have compacted it still more, wearing it into a smooth or slippery surface.

☐ Provision should be made for a practice, or 'riding-in', area near by. When choosing such a site, bear in mind how many horses are likely to be using it at one time so that there is enough good, level ground available.

☐ The amount of land required will depend on how many arenas will be used at the same time in the same area. Allow a 20-metre space between each arena, to minimise the possibility of distraction or interference.

☐ Remember to leave enough space for the judges' vehicles, which should be positioned about 2 metres beyond the 'C' marker.

☐ To protect the arena from the public a minimum area of 10 metres should be left surrounding it. Competitors may use this area for last-minute preparations before their test begins. If there is likely to be a large number of spectators and/or cars around the arena, 20 metres would be a safer distance.

LAYING OUT AN ARENA

There are many different ways of setting out a dressage arena, but this task will be much simpler, and quicker, if you acquire or make a special device for the purpose. You will need:
(a) A piece of non-stretchable tape or rope. For a small arena (20 × 40 metres) it should be 120 metres long; for a large arena (20 × 60 metres), 160 metres long. Starting at the first corner, carefully measure out and mark the tape with bright paint to show each letter and corner. The tape will be easy to deal with if rolled on to a large reel with a handle or mechanical device. Remember that when making a 20 × 60 metre arena the distance between each marker must be adjusted.
(b) A measure 40 metres long, and a piece of string 15 metres long.

Method

1. Make a loop at the beginning of the string and stake it in the ground with a 10 cm (4 in) nail.
2. Measure out 3 metres from the first loop, and make a second loop.
3. Measure out 4 metres, and make a third loop.
4. Measure a further 5 metres from the third loop, and join the end to the first loop.
The piece of string, stretched out tight and held by nails in the three loops at each point, will form a right-angled triangle, based on the Pythagoras principle, as shown.

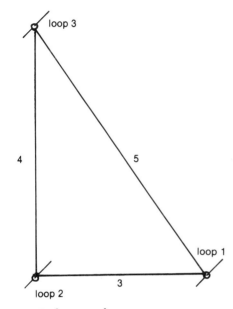

loop 3

4

5

loop 1

loop 2

3

Pythagoras theory.

SETTING UP A SMALL ARENA (20 m × 40 m)

1. Select your area for the arena, and knock in the corner peg.
2. Stake the second loop of your triangular string, at the corner peg.
3. Stretch the string tight and stake the first loop along the intended line of the short side of the arena.
4. Measure out 20 metres and knock in the second corner peg.
5. Pull tight the 4 metre length of string, up to the third loop, and stake it.
6. Measure out 40 metres down and beyond this length and knock in the third corner peg.
7. Now transverse the triangle to make a right-angled corner at the other end of the existing 20 metre side, again using the second loop at the corner peg, and the first loop pulled back towards the original peg.
8. Stretch the triangle tight and measure down and beyond it for 40 metres, to get the final corner peg.
9. Check that the distance between the pegs at the end of the two 40-metre sides is 20 metres exactly. It will probably need slight adjustment.

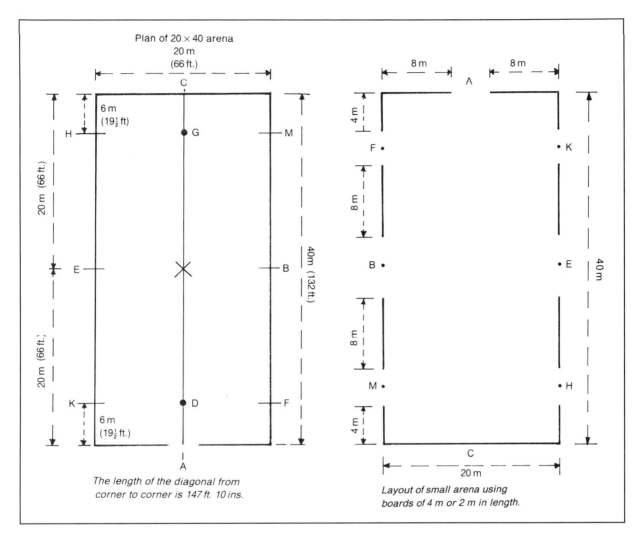

The length of the diagonal from corner to corner is 147 ft. 10 ins.

Layout of small arena using boards of 4 m or 2 m in length.

10. You now have the four corners, and can fill in the sides with the surrounding barrier and letter markers. (This is where the specially prepared 120-metre tape will prove an invaluable time saver.)

SETTING UP A LARGE ARENA (20 m × 60 m)

Extend the lengths at stages 6 and 8 (above) by a further 20 metres, and adjust the position of each letter, which should be marked out on the 160 m reel of tape.

Remember to leave a gap for the entrance to the arena at A. It should be at least 2 metres wide (1 metre on either side of the centre line.) The letter marker at A should be positioned far back enough to allow for a straight entry from left or right. Alternatively, two white posts can be used to mark the entrance.

At the lower levels, a centre line is not essential, but it will be appreciated by competitors and will help the judge. To mow a path of, say, 18 in (46 cm) width, stretch a length of tape or rope approximately 12 in (30 cm) to one side of the centre line between markers A and C, and use this length as a guide to keep the mower straight. If an all-weather surface type of arena is being used, the line can be rolled, but it will need renewing at frequent intervals. When no machinery is available, sawdust or white paint may be used to mark either side of points D, X and G, leaving an avenue. These markings should remain in place throughout the competition, as the horses may pass between each pair, guiding them in a straight line. It is a mistake to put a glaring white blob right on the centre line — horses will shy away from it, or jump it.

Materials

□ The arena edge should be defined clearly and accurately, and there is a wide choice of materials available for making the surround. Among the most practical are wooden boards, built in an inverted V-shape and held together by crosspieces at each end. They are easy to position, and can be placed over the line or rope marking out the area, which can then be pulled away and re-wound. Some boards have small protruding 'legs' which can be adapted to uneven ground: without legs, one end is apt to rise if there is a bump.

Single wooden boards may be attached to pointed posts made of wood or metal. These are easy to adjust to a level height and to straighten, and they are particularly suitable for rough or uneven ground. Boards may also be propped up on metal pins, like tent pegs, which should be attached to the outside. All low boards should lean outward slightly, to minimise the risk if horses tread on them. Stake them in firmly with pegs on the outside, or lean them against props. Whichever material you choose, it must not break or move easily. Straight lines must be maintained. Boards may be continuous or intermittent, but it is important for the corners to be strongly defined. A simple layout is using boards 4 metres long, with marker posts positioned in the gaps.

The disadvantages of wood are (1) it needs regular painting and maintenance, as it tends to warp and rot, and (2) it can also be damaged during stacking and transporting.

Plastic provides some useful alternatives, though in wet, muddy conditions it tends to discolour. White plastic tape, attached to posts and raised 2 in to 6 in (5 cm to 15 cm) above the ground, makes a continuous and consistent surround. It must be set up carefully so that it cannot bend or wave in the wind. Plastic guttering is practical and easy to store and carry, but it is only suitable on level ground. Prefabricated solid plastic boards are popular because they are resilient, longer-lasting than wood, light and easy to store. Like wooden boards, they are only suitable for even ground unless they have 'legs'.

More elaborate surrounds, are used for major competitions, when a higher, continuous barrier is essential for competitors and judges. □ Under British Rules, a competitor who leaves the arena during a

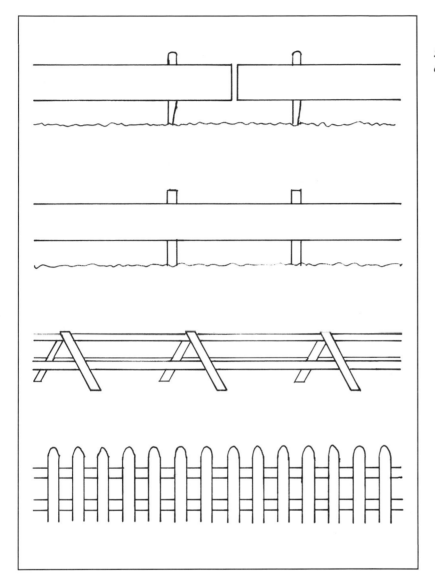

Some types of boarding for dressage arenas.

test when the surround is 9 in (23 cm) high or more is eliminated. However, when the surround is lower, or not continuous, marks will be deducted. In the United States, and under FEI Rules, the surround may be 1 ft (0.30 m) or even higher; but leaving the arena (all four feet outside the arena's perimeter), entails elimination.

□ The letter markers, usually painted black on a white background, are placed outside the arena approximately 20 in (0.50 m) from the white marker post. If this post is on the outside of the boards, it must show about 6 in (15 cm) above them so that riders and judges may see the exact spot clearly. Inaccuracy can cost a competitor valuable marks. In the US, the post is painted red, 8 in (20 cm) high, and placed inside and against the arena surround. The letters can be

A well laid-out dressage arena.

painted on to square wooden or metal boards staked in the ground. Upturned buckets, plastic cones, or wooden cubes are useful alternatives. Remember that they are subjected to frequent stacking, storing and transporting.

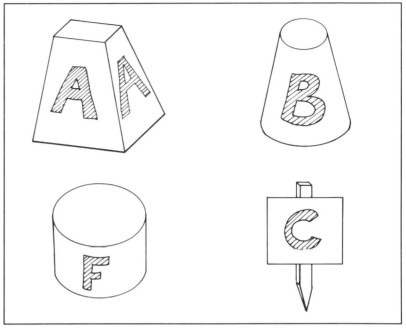

Types of dressage marker.

☐ The surface of the arena should be as consistent as possible. This may involve rolling the ground, or in extreme cases, watering it. Where the grass has grown too tall and rank it may need 'topping' or mowing: but do not cut it too short so that it could be slippery or bare. Long grass tends to impede the freedom of a horse's action, and may obscure the surrounding boards or tape.

☐ Decoration: Pot plants, shrubs, or flowers add to the elegance of a dressage display or performance. They set the stage, and are particularly fitting on a big occasion, when competitors are dressed up in top hats and tail coats.

Judges

☐ At Event dressage competitions, judges usually mark tests sitting in a car. This has the advantage of being virtually soundproof, dry and comfortable, and provides a convenient passenger seat for the writer.

☐ When only one judge is required, the vehicle must be carefully parked so that he, or she, can see straight down the centre line.

In Britain, when there are two judges for one arena, they are positioned close together on either side of the prolongation of the centre line. In the US, when two judges are used, one is placed at C, and the other either at H or M, 2 m to 5 m from, and on the inside of the prolongation of the long sides.

☐ In informal types of competition and those run in hot weather, judges may be inclined to sit out in the open air, using a table and chairs. This is not ideal, since horses will tend to shy or spook, especially when papers rustle, for example. Also, the judges' comments may be audible. Large sunshades or umbrellas should not be used.

☐ Major competitions or those held on permanent dressage sites may be judged from specially built judges' boxes. These are usually wooden, and must provide an unrestricted view of the arena. When there are three or five judges, the principal one is positioned at C, 5 metres outside the arena. Judges at M and H should be 2 to 5 metres in from and on the inside of the prolongation of the long sides. If further judges are placed at B and E, they should be 5 metres outside the arena, opposite the markers.

Part 3
SHOW JUMPING

Show Jumping

1. THE COURSE DESIGNER'S BRIEF

The show jumping phase of an Event must be treated as part of the overall competition, and not as a separate class. It should be designed to have the correct influence on the final result, in relation to the cross-country and dressage phases.

The success or failure of a course should not be assessed on the number of clear rounds jumped but on the effect that it has on the final placings. As a guide, the show jumping phase should only exert one-twelfth of the influence of the cross-country phase, and one-third of the dressage phase. To achieve this balance nothing should be left to chance, and organisers of Events at any level should employ a recognised designer, as a bad course will alter or spoil a competition by producing a false result. The designer's other main role is to encourage and to assist in the training of the horse and the rider as they progress through the grades. An unhappy experience in the show jumping arena can destroy months of training, and can damage a horse's confidence or even cause serious injury. Above all, a course must be safe to ride and enjoyable to jump.

Never try to copy a course which has worked well at another Event. Every situation is unique. Factors to be considered include the standard of competition, the size and shape of the arena, its terrain and, of course, the weather.

Anyone aspiring to be a successful designer and builder of courses should ask to be an assistant to as many recognised designers as possible. This way you will learn how to understand each problem.

2. THE ARENA

The show jumping arena must be sited on the best available area of ground. Flat ground is ideal, although gentle gradients are acceptable. The arena should be as close as possible to other areas of activity, allowing easy access, communications and emergency services. It should not, however, interfere with any of the other phases.

The recommended minimum size of an arena is 300 ft × 250 ft

(90 m × 75 m), but it does not have to be rectangular. A larger arena will be more appropriate for a major Event. A warm-up area large enough to accommodate two practice fences must be provided near the collecting ring. Where space is limited it should be roped off for safety.

Spectators will appreciate being able to park their cars around the arena. At major Events special areas may be reserved for sponsors, and for Members if such a scheme is operated. A refreshment tent near the arena will provide a view-point and a shelter in bad weather, while an area which forms a natural grandstand or amphitheatre can be used to the advantage of spectators in fine weather.

The arena must be enclosed. This can be done with a single rope on posts, or with more elaborate fencing. Never use pig wire, barbed wire, or anything in which a loose horse could entangle itself.

To make the surface as even as possible, areas of coarse long grass, thistles and nettles should be cut down. If the grass is mown a few days in advance it will have a chance of 'greening up' for the day, and will make a better surface for riding. Long grass can be slippery in wet weather. If the ground is hard and if irrigation is not available, sand or a similar substance should be laid on both the take-off and landing sides of each fence.

Ground which tends to become deep and boggy in wet weather should be avoided.

3. EQUIPMENT AND MATERIALS

Events which do not have their own show jumps will need to order a set in advance, along with the timing equipment if necessary. The course designer should be consulted as to the items and material required. For a *10 fence course* you will require: *24 pairs of wings*. This allows for two combinations, plus 3 pairs for the practice fences, and spares in case of breakages on the day. *40 poles* should be adequate, provided that there are at least *6 sets of fillers* (such as walls, hurdles, brushes), a *set of planks*, and *a gate*.

There must be enough *cups* for the poles. 'Flat' cups are needed for the planks and gates. You will also need a *set of numbers* and *'Start'* and *'Finish' boards*, Depending on the rules of the particular competition, *flags* may also be required for each fence and for the start and finish.

If the Event provides its own jumps, checks should be made to ensure that there will be enough material, that they are in a good state of repair, that they are painted, and that any wing nuts are oiled.

The judges must have a clear view of the entire area. A box or caravan is far more satisfactory than a motor car. A specially adapted or purpose-made caravan can be hired.

Communications for the show jumping phase should be separate from the main public address system. The flow of the competition will also be improved if the collecting ring steward has two-way radio or land-phone communication with both the judges' box or commentator and the practice area. Even the smallest Event should have a megaphone available.

Trees For Decoration will improve the appearance of a course, if you can afford them. They will obviously have to be ordered in advance. A pair of trees per fence is adequate, though more may be preferred. The Christmas tree spruce, 4 ft to 5 ft (1.2 m to 1.5 m) in height, is the most suitable. A local nursery or garden centre may be willing to loan or rent out some plants in return for a free advertisement in the programme or at the side of the arena.

The more that can be organised in advance, the fewer problems should arise on the day.

4. OFFICIALS

The level of the competition and the number or entries will determine how many officials will be required. They should be commissioned well in advance and should consist of:

THE COURSE DESIGNER, who should be encouraged to bring an assistant as a trainee for future events.

THE JUDGE, a TIMEKEEPER JUDGE and a WRITER.

A COMMENTATOR, COLLECTING RING STEWARD and ASSISTANT.

AN ARENA PARTY. A minimum of four people will be required, though more would be an advantage if there is to be change of course during the day, if the arena is large, or if the competition is likely to last a long time. It is an advantage if you can arrange to have the same people who helped to build the course. A local scout group or military organisation is often willing to help out for a nominal donation towards their expenses and funds. The course designer should advise as to when the arena party will be required and for how long. Remember that the course has to be taken down at the end of the day!

All officials and voluntary helpers will need some refreshment, especially if it is a cold day. Frequent dispensation of hot tea or coffee is minimal repayment for their services, which are often given free. For a long day you may need to organise some relief helpers.

5. PLANNING AND DESIGNING THE COURSE

The designer should obtain as much information as possible in advance. He will need to check the requirements of the scheduled classes in the relevant rule book, which can change from year to year. The rule book may give the minimum and maximum length of the course, the number of jumps or the type of combinations, maximum heights and spreads, and other information. It is not advisable to incorporate water, ditches or banks into an Event show jumping course, as a horse will see plenty of these on the cross-country; a water tray could be used in an Advanced class.

If you have not previously built a course at a particular Event, obtain from the organiser the size of the arena, the positions of the entrance and exit, and any permanent features within the arena, such as trees and water. If possible visit the site in advance, especially if it is a new Event, when advice may be offered.

The number of expected entries and time allowed for this phase may determine that the length of the course will need to be kept to the minimum.

A list of the items of fence material, and the name of the supplier, will also be useful for your pre-planning.

With all the necessary information at hand, plan your course on paper. Graph paper is preferable, as you can use the squares to correspond with a scale. A knowledge of basic drawing techniques and scales can be useful at this stage. Another practical aid is a table top, with matchsticks as fences and string to outline the arena.

A plan should work on paper first. However, always be prepared to be flexible once you arrive at the site, as circumstances are not always as you expect them.

A separate course will be required for each class. Plan the most important, (e.g. the Advanced) first, so that the other classes can then be incorporated within it. Try not to have any predetermined ideas of which fences are to be spreads or combinations. Just draw single lines. Nine numbered fences for most classes will be adequate to obtain the result required unless the rules call for more. Jumping the last fence towards the exit, will save time on the day of the Event.

It will encourage horses (especially in Novice classes) to jump the first two fences towards the entrance. Fences built *too* close to the entrance or exit, may tempt them to run out. If possible allow at least 90 ft (27 m) between both the approach and landing side of a fence and the end of the arena. Each fence should be set 20 ft (6 m) in from the side. In a Novice class there should be at least one change of direction but more need to be incorporated in an Advanced class to provide the requisite test of the horse's suppleness and obedience. If space allows, each fence should be at least six non-jumping strides (84 ft, 26 m) apart. A more advanced course can include two fences on a shorter distance, which again should be measured in multiples of 12ft (3.5 m) — an average horse's stride. A curving line between fences, rather than a straight one, will allow a rider to adjust a horse's stride.

On your plan, link up each fence with a pencil line, following the route that an average rider would take, to ensure that there are no sharp turns and that one fence will not be in the way of another.

Having planned the first course, mark the fence numbers with a coloured pen and draw an arrow to show the direction in which the fences are to be jumped. Use the same procedure for the other courses, with different coloured pens for each class.

There is no reason why the course should not be designed so that a fence can be jumped in the opposite direction in another class, but try to restrict these to uprights such as walls and gates, which will require the minimum of adjustment to turn them around. If there is spare material this can be incorporated into a second course as a different fence, but it will need to be crossed off on the day when not in use.

Once the basic course has been designed, you can decide the position of the combinations and which fences will be uprights or spreads. The latter two should be on a fifty/fifty ratio, evenly distributed around the course. Remember to avoid spreads out of tight corners and away from the entrance of the arena as these can be difficult to jump.

Combinations

Even if the rules do not stipulate it, a combination should be included in every course. A combination is either a 'double', or 'treble', — two or three efforts with one or two non-jumping strides between them. Most rule books stipulate the minimum and maximum distances to be used. Each combination is numbered as one fence, with each effort marked (A), (B) or (C) on the course plan, and on the side of the fence itself if the rules require it.

For a Novice Event, one 'double' combination (two fences) in the second half of the course will be adequate. A more advanced class could incorporate either a double and a treble or two doubles. It is easier to jump a double before a treble. A good guide is to have the double not before Fence 4 and the treble not before Fence 7.

As a two-strided combination is easier to jump than a single-strided one, this will be preferable for a Novice class.

Wherever a spread fence is built for the second or third part of a combination it should have a two-strided distance before it, to enable a horse to jump it more easily.

If two combinations are to be included, a variation in their construction will make the course more interesting, with the easier of the two in the first part of the course — for example, an upright before a spread with two non-jumping strides between them, followed by a spread to an upright on one non-jumping stride. A wall or gate should never be used as part of a combination for safety reasons, and it is not advisable to include a triple bar, except for the most advanced competitions and then only if the course designer is very experienced.

The tables on pages 212/3 give suggested permissible maximum and minimum distances in combinations for Horse Trials, built on level ground with perfect going. The final distance should not be decided until the day of the competition, after you have inspected the ground and know more about the likely standard of the competitors.

Remember that a Novice horse over a 3 ft (91 cm) course will land shorter into a combination than an Advanced horse over a 4 ft (1.2 m) course.

For ponies, with their shorter strides, the distances must be shortened by 18 ins (46 cm) for one non-jumping stride and 2 ft 6 in (76 cm) to 3 ft (91 cm) for two non-jumping strides. Because the length of stride can vary so much between breeds and types, *always* use two non-jumping strides on the approach to an oxer when it is either the second or third part of a combination.

It is impossible to lay down exact distances between fences. A course designer must use his or her own judgement and not try to be clever and set 'traps'. Hard or deep going, uphill gradients, and fences away from the arena entrance tend to shorten a horse's stride, while the opposite will apply to a horse going towards 'home', downhill or on perfect going. Only experience can help you decide how to adjust for these circumstances, but if you are in any doubt the best advice is always to finish a line with a vertical and not a spread. This way, if the line becomes too long or too short, a horse will only roll the top

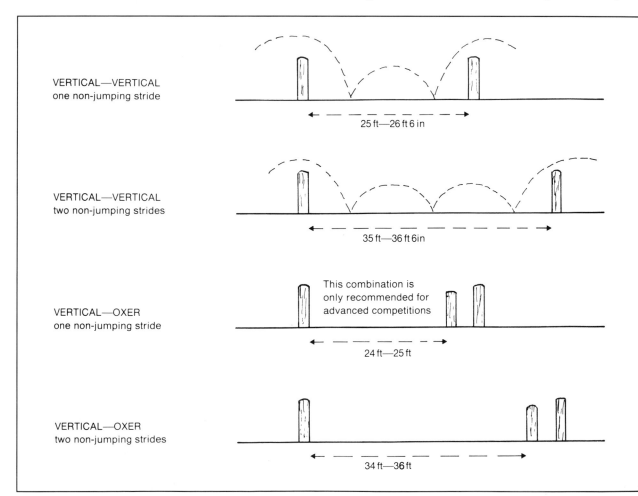

VERTICAL—VERTICAL
one non-jumping stride

25 ft—26 ft 6 in

VERTICAL—VERTICAL
two non-jumping strides

35 ft—36 ft 6in

VERTICAL—OXER
one non-jumping stride

This combination is
only recommended for
advanced competitions

24 ft—25 ft

VERTICAL—OXER
two non-jumping strides

34 ft—36 ft

Table of distances in combinations

Recommended distances between fences in combinations, built on level ground, with perfect going, for horses taking part in Horse Trials.

This chart should only be used as a guide. Take into consideration the points already made before deciding on distances, the actual type of combination to build and the distances to use, and what adjustments to make for ponies (see page 212). ● A treble combination should be built as a one non jumping stride to a two non jumping stride, and not the other way around. ● The distances should be as precise as possible. ● Never build a 'long' distance to a 'short' distance. ● An ascending oxer to a one-strided vertical to an ascending or square oxer on two strides would be suitable for an Advanced class. For Intermediate level, or below, it would be more appropriate to make the third part a vertical. ● Never include three 'spread' fences in a treble combination. ● For courses below 3 ft (90 cm) in height the distances can be shortened by 6 in (15 cm) for a one non jumping stride and 12 in (30 cm) for a two non jumping stride combination. At this level of competition a two-stride combination is recommended. ● To maintain a constant level of competition throughout the course the heights of the combinations should be set 2 in or 3 in (5 cm or 8 cm) below the maximum height of the rest of the course.

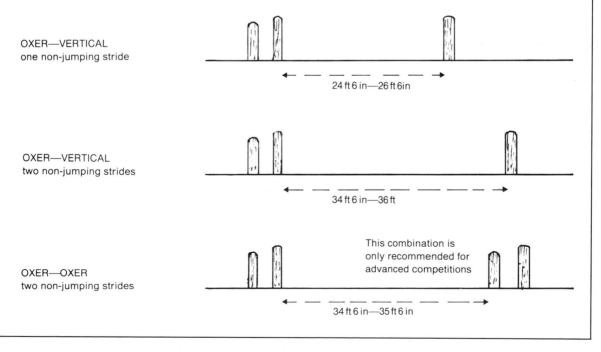

OXER—VERTICAL
one non-jumping stride

24 ft 6 in—26 ft 6in

OXER—VERTICAL
two non-jumping strides

34 ft 6 in—36 ft

OXER—OXER
two non-jumping strides

This combination is only recommended for advanced competitions

34 ft 6 in—35 ft 6 in

Example of a draft course plan

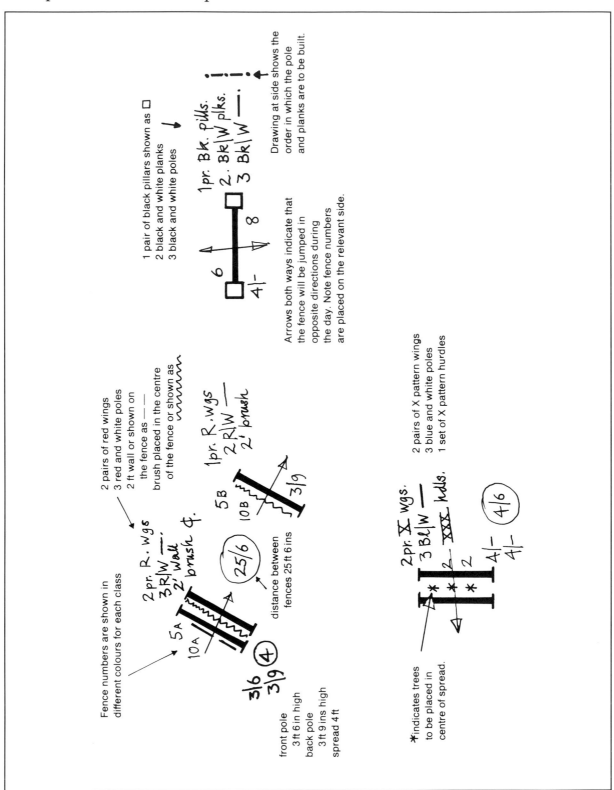

1 pair of black pillars shown as ▢
2 black and white planks
3 black and white poles

Drawing at side shows the order in which the pole and planks are to be built.

1pr. Bk. pills.
2. Bk|W plks.
3 Bk|W —

Arrows both ways indicate that the fence will be jumped in opposite directions during the day. Note fence numbers are placed on the relevant side.

2 pairs of red wings
3 red and white poles
2 ft wall or shown on the fence as ——
brush placed in the centre of the fence or shown as ∿∿∿

1pr. R. wgs
2 R|W —
2' brush

2 pr. R. wgs
3 R|W —
2' wall
brush ¢.

Fence numbers are shown in different colours for each class

distance between fences 25ft 6ins

front pole 3ft 6in high
back pole 3ft 9ins high
spread 4ft

2 pairs of X pattern wings
3 blue and white poles
1 set of X pattern hurdles

2pr. X wgs.
3 Bl|W —
2 XXX hdls.
2

*indicates trees to be placed in centre of spread.

214

Example of completed course plan for a major horse trial

DATE *29 September 1985*

EVENT *Chesterland Three-Day Event*

CLASS *1. C. C. I*

DISTANCE *800 metres*   SPEED *400 m/min.*

TIME ALLOWED *2 minutes*   TIME LIMIT *4 mins.*

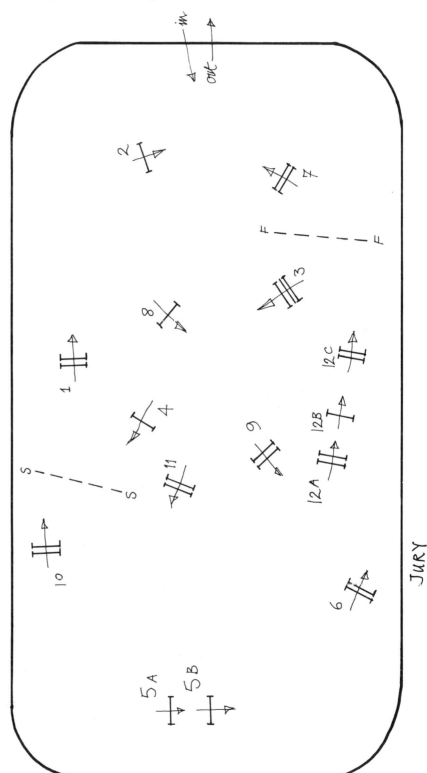

JURY

pole off rather than crashing into the centre of a spread fence.

As a general guide for horses, on flat, perfect going, fences should be spaced apart by multiple distances of 12 ft. This follows the average stride of a horse. Because Event horses spend a lot of their time galloping over cross-country courses, they are inclined to take longer strides than pure show jumpers, who tend to be more collected in the jumping arena. A course designer may feel it necessary to allow for this when deciding on the distance to use.

For ponies, a multiple of 11 ft (3.3 m) would be more appropriate. Never place two jumps any closer than 77 ft (23 m) as a bold, long-striding pony may cover the distance in one stride fewer than a shorter-striding pony.

With your list of fence materials at hand you can now decide on the construction of each fence, incorporating all this information

An inviting first fence. A pair of short standards are used to support the low rustic gate. Two poles are placed on the back pillars, but note that the lower one is still higher than the front element. Shrubs, in plastic, not metal, containers, are used to fill the spread. The front element would have benefited from two additional shrubs placed on each side of the standards.

into your draft course plan. You can avoid confusion by using a coloured pen to correspond with the colour of the poles.

The first fence should always be built to look as inviting as possible, and must not be a true upright. It should have a well defined groundline and sloping front.

Combinations look better if all the parts or elements are of the same material and the same colour.

Try to distribute the colours of the other fences evenly around the course. Any sponsored fences should, if possible, be placed in a prominent position.

TYPES OF JUMP

Show jumps are either verticals, oxers, or triple bars. A vertical is generally referred to as an 'upright' while the other two are 'spreads'.

The following are some of the different ways in which fences can be constructed. They become progressively more difficult, though they will vary a little depending on the circumstances of each jump, its exact situation, and its relation to the remainder of the course.

Verticals
(a) Poles with a wall or brush set in front of them.
(b) Poles set over the centre of a wall or brush.
(c) Poles set flush to the face of a wall, hurdle, hanging panel, or small gate.
(d) Wall with rounded 'tops'.
(e) Wall with square 'tops'.
(f) Poles and planks, with a pole as the top element.
(g) Poles only.
(h) Gate.
(i) Poles and planks, with a plank as the top element.
(j) Planks only.

Oxers
It is assumed that the following are all ascending oxers (i.e. the front pole is lower than the back pole). If both poles are built at the same height they form a 'true' oxer, which is more difficult.
(a) Poles with a wall or brush set in front of, or centred under, the front pole.
(b) Poles with a wall, hurdle, hanging panel, or gate set flush with the front pole.
(c) Poles only (setting a brush in the centre between front and back poles could form a false groundline, but trees could fill in the centre and make it easier).
(d) A gate or plank as the top element of the front with ONE POLE set behind.

217

Fence types

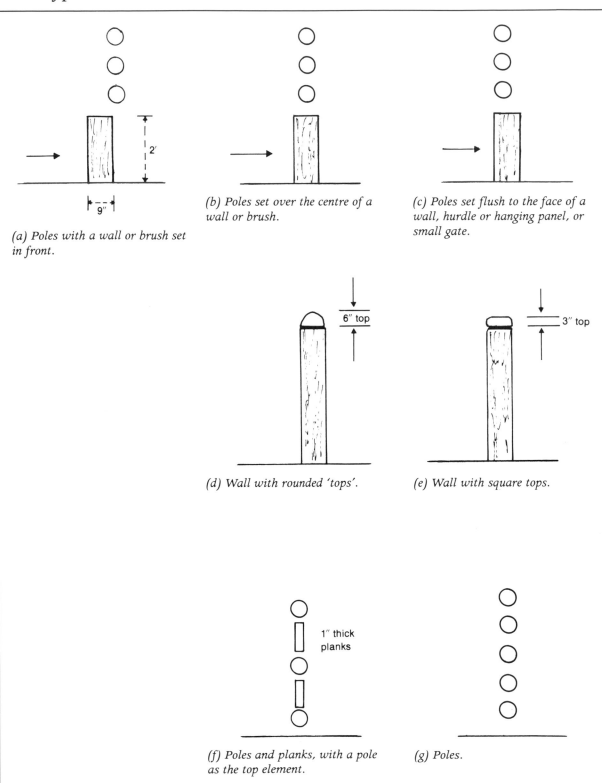

(a) Poles with a wall or brush set in front.

(b) Poles set over the centre of a wall or brush.

(c) Poles set flush to the face of a wall, hurdle or hanging panel, or small gate.

(d) Wall with rounded 'tops'.

(e) Wall with square tops.

(f) Poles and planks, with a pole as the top element.

(g) Poles.

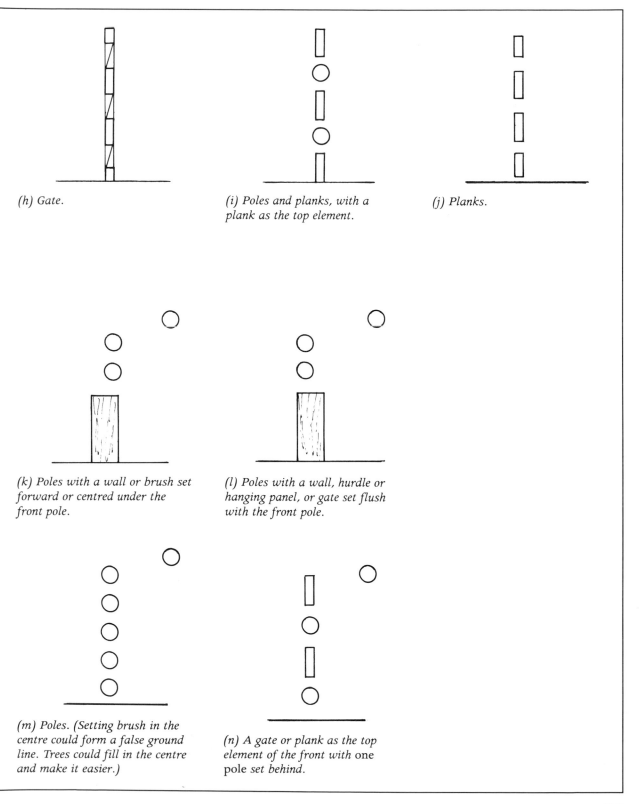

(h) Gate.

(i) Poles and planks, with a plank as the top element.

(j) Planks.

(k) Poles with a wall or brush set forward or centred under the front pole.

(l) Poles with a wall, hurdle or hanging panel, or gate set flush with the front pole.

(m) Poles. (Setting brush in the centre could form a false ground line. Trees could fill in the centre and make it easier.)

(n) A gate or plank as the top element of the front with one pole set behind.

Triple Bars

These usually consist of three sets of wing standards, but two sets may sometimes be used, with either (a) a small wall or brush as the first element (in which case two trees or a pair of small pillars should be set at the side as wings) or (b) a brush as the middle element, which must be higher than the front pole. The front element should be kept low enough to prevent the fence becoming too 'flat'. A triple bar should never be concave — that is to say the middle element should always be level with or slightly above a line formed by laying your measuring staff on the front and back pole. It may be necessary to place two poles on the centre pair of wings to make the fence more solid — but never use more than two poles and always keep at least a 6 in (15 cm) gap between them, with the lower pole at the same height, or higher than, the top front pole. A small brush, or shrubs, placed between the first two pairs of wings will give the fences a more solid appearance.

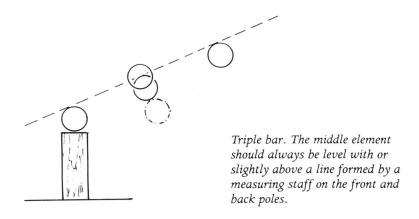

Triple bar. The middle element should always be level with or slightly above a line formed by a measuring staff on the front and back poles.

Notes

Fences should always be built to look as solid as possible, with a groundline to encourage good jumping. However, if a pole is used to provide the groundline, always ensure that it is fixed with pegs, otherwise it can roll if a horse places a foot on it, which is dangerous. In an Advanced competition it would be permissible to include one more 'open' type of fence in the course, but this should never be the first fence or part of a combination.

☐ The normal length of a show jumping pole is 12 ft (3.6 m). Occasionally a set of 'style' poles (6 ft to 8 ft or 1.8 m to 2.4 m) is included with the fences delivered to the site. These are best left on the trailer for use in standard show jumping competitions.

☐ Always ensure that any gates or large panels used as the front element of an oxer will fall easily (flat cups are essential)

Only *one pole* (never a plank) should be placed on the back element.

Time can be saved on building day, if you have a provisional idea of the heights and widths of the fences and the distances between them, these measurements should only be a guide; the final decisions must be made once you have arrived on the site and assessed the ground.

☐ The first two fences and the combinations should be one or two holes lower than the remainder of the course. At least half of the fences on the course should measure up to the maximum dimensions stipulated in the rules for the particular class.

☐ To retain good proportions and to encourage good jumping the spread of a fence should measure between one and one and a half times the height of the fence. Anything any wider should have a brush or shrubs placed through the centre to fill it in. A spread fence with both the front and back pole at the same height is far more difficult to jump than one with a lower front pole. Therefore a 'true' oxer should only be used as an individual fence with a good approach, and must be used with discretion in a Novice class.

6. BUILDING THE COURSE

The course builder should arrive on site in advance of the arena party. A detailed plan, using an inventory of jump material, will help to save time and preclude fences having to be rebuilt or redesigned.

If there is a shortage of anything, it is likely to be fillers. Straw bales give a good solid groundline at the base of the fence. Alternatively, barrels can be used, but they should be plastic or wood, and *not metal*, for safety reasons. They should be laid end to end, with a pole secured to the ground on either side to prevent them from rolling should a horse slide into them or should the wind blow them. Trimmings from hedges or branches from trees can help make fences more inviting. If there is a great shortage of material, an upright fence marked with two separate numbers can be jumped twice, possibly in opposite directions. It must be near to the beginning and the end of the course to allow time for rebuilding should it be knocked down.

Begin setting out the course either by placing poles on the ground, or if you feel more confident, by putting the numbers in the relative position of each fence as shown on your plan. Once the pole for the first fence has been laid, walk on to where the next fence will be, in multiples of four human paces (12 ft or 3.6 m). Lay the pole in the correct position, and so on. You can practise walking this at home by marking two points, say 72 ft (21.9 m) apart, and striding it every time you pass until you are happy that you can walk in paces of 3 ft (91 cm). When you walk a bending line, always proceed 12 paces (36 ft, 10.9 m) straight on from the centre of the last fence before you start to turn. You must always walk the route that the horse is likely to take on the day.

When the rules require a class to be of a certain length, now is the time to check. At this stage you can adjust the position of poles or the length of course as necessary without moving whole fences.

If the pole placed on the ground is the same colour as intended for the finished obstacle (with two poles laid side by side where it is to be an oxer) it will help anyone bringing out the rest of the material to recognise the fence.

Having 'outlined' the course to your satisfaction you can now proceed to build it. If you have an assistant and an arena party, you can form two groups — one to bring in the equipment and the other to help with the building. If a vehicle with a trailer is available the job will be quicker and easier, but in wet weather when the ground is soft a vehicle should not be used in the arena, as its tracks will spoil the surface, and any deep ruts could be dangerous to the competitors. Instead, the vehicle should be driven around the outside of the arena, dropping off the fence equipment at the appropriate points.

At this stage, build to the heights and spreads that you have planned in advance. Always use a wooden staff or ruler marked in feet and inches or metres and centimetres. A metal tape invariably bends and therefore does not provide an accurate measurement.

A triple bar constructed with only two pairs of wings. The wall is brought forward to form the front element, with shrubs as 'wings'.

Begin by positioning the top pole. Place the cup-pins in the holes from front to back, pointing in the same direction as that in which the horse will jump the fence. This helps to prevent cups falling off if the fence is knocked over. Having placed the pole at the correct

height (and spread in the case of an oxer, which should be measured from the outer edges of the two pairs of wings on each side), fill in with the remainder of the material, spacing the poles evenly. If you do not have machined poles, and if the ground slopes, the thick ends of the poles should be positioned downhill. Ensure that the face of any filler is not behind the vertical plane of the poles, which would give a false groundline. For safety, never use anything but one pole on the back of an oxer, and always ensure that it is not lower than the front pole. Gates and planks must always be placed on flat cups. This is most important when they form the top element of a fence.

The fence number should be positioned on the right-hand side of the obstacle. If the course has to be flagged, place the white flag on the left-hand side and the red flag on the right. Some fences will have holes or brackets for flags. On others, freestanding flags will have to be used. They must always be placed as near as possible to the end of the pole or other item to be jumped. If placed on the outside of a

An oxer with a well-defined groundline. The back pole is clearly visible above the filling and the top front pole. The matched trees on the front wings will help to prevent a horse from running out, as well as being decorative.

freestanding pillar they will be subject to penalty and will be scored as such if they are knocked over, even if the rest of the fence remains standing. Oxers and triple bars should be flagged on both front and back elements. If there are not enough flags to go around, just flagging the rear element will be adequate. Flags or markers will also be needed for the Start and Finish.

Having drawn out the distance for the 'flat' on paper in advance, you must now make necessary allowances for gradient, and the state of the going. Remember that any variation from a 12 ft (3.6 m) distance will, in addition to the above factors, prevent the course from 'flowing' comfortably for the competitors.

The distance between each element of a combination must always be measured from the back of the first element to the front of the next one. Tape to the front of the top pole cup and not to the front of a pillar or a projecting filler.

For safety reasons, always ensure that there are no sharp objects or

A jump designed for the Badminton Horse Trials, showing how a basic wall and a pair of pillars can become a realistic-looking 'public house' by using paint.

The wall is in two sections, with the rooftop in six pieces so that it will fall easily should a horse go through it. The top element is a pole painted to match the 'roof', and it is resting on a cup. The fence is finished with decorations appropriate to a 'pub' setting (although the umbrella should be removed on a windy day). Note the correct positions of the flags on the inside edge of the pillars.

nails sticking out, and that gates and planks have the 'nut' side of any metal brackets facing away from the approach to the fence.

When the course has been built, remove all spare equipment from within the arena and store it neatly near by. Always have on hand one spare pole of each colour in case of breakages, and brief the arena party as to their whereabouts.

Branches attached to wings can make the course look more attractive, but make sure that they are secure and that no sharp ends project. Sawn trees or shrubs will need to have their ends pointed and should be inserted in deep holes made with an iron bar so that they will not blow over. Small trees or shrubs can be placed through the centre of oxers to make them look more solid, but trim off any tops which show above the back pole. Plants on loan should not be placed behind wings, as they can be damaged if a wing is knocked over.

Now is the time to recheck the height and spread of each fence and, if you consider that any of your initial calculations were wrong, to make the appropriate adjustments. The length of the course must then be measured with a wheel, taking the route of an average competitor, and not cutting the corners or going to the ends of the arena unnecessarily.

Before the course is 'opened' to the competitors for walking (generally at least one hour before the start of the show jumping phase) it must be inspected and approved by the Official Steward, or Technical Delegate, who has the power to make any necessary alteration. The judges should also be escorted round and any unusual features, such as faultable fillers, should be pointed out.

A final course-plan must be prepared. At the top of the plan give the name of the Event, the date, and the class. The plan should show as closely as possibly the relative position of each fence, with arrows indicating the direction in which they are to be jumped, and their numbers, including an A, B or C in the case of a combination. Any fences in the arena which are not to be used in the particular class should be shown by just a dotted line. The entrance and exit, position of the judges, and Start and Finish line must also be included. Details must be given of the distance of the course, the speed at which it is to be ridden, the time allowed (calculated from tables included in most rule books), and the time limit (twice the time allowed). The plan for Chesterland shown on page 215 illustrates this.

If possible, make carbon or photocopies of your original plan. This will prevent the kind of error which can occur when each copy is drawn separately.

One copy of the plan must be posted close to the entrance of the arena before the course is 'opened'. The judges must also be given a copy. The Steward (or Technical Delegate), the designer, and any assistants should have copies on which should be noted the heights, spreads and distances of the fences for reference in case they are dislodged.

Before the jumping starts, the arena party must be briefed as to how and when to rebuild a fence, and what to do if a horse when refusing dislodges part of a fence. If planks or gates on flat cups, and wall bricks are tapped by the horses they must be checked for correct positioning. Any emergency drill must be practised, and the rule on outside assistance must be made clear.

If the ground cuts up badly, a fence can be resited between classes. At the same time, if you consider a distance is riding very badly, you can adjust it, but always discuss it first with the Steward or Technical Delegate and have it announced to the competitors, allowing them the chance to rewalk it.

If time allows, try to keep a record of the number of knockdowns at fences where they occur, by writing them in on your course plan. Alternatively, obtain copies of the judges' score sheets at the end of the day. On a successful course the first and possibly the second fence should show hardly any faults, and penalties should be evenly distributed around the remainder of the course. If the distribution is not even, or if one particular fence has caused an excessive number of refusals — try to assess the reasons. For example, the position of the sun as the day progresses can cause difficulties, as can the use of a wrong distance; eventualities such as these should be taken into account when planning a course.

On a good course there is no 'bogey' fence. Faults are kept to a minimum and, although accidents *can* happen, no horse or rider should be hurt because of failings by the course designer or builder.

Making Your Own Show Jumps

Safety is the most important factor. With this in mind, there must be no sharp edges or points which can injure a horse or rider if they collide with a jump or wing stand. All metal edges must be smooth. Bolts should be cut back to the nut, and any nails that protrude should be bent over and knocked flat.

Though treated softwood is expensive, it is well worth the investment if you want your fences to last. For the same reason, only superior quality plywood should be used.

The standard length of a pole is 12 ft (3.6 m) with an average diameter of 4 in (10 cms). Poles cut from a plantation are adequate for use when schooling, but poles purchased from a timber supplier which have been 'machined' to the same diameter for their entire length are more suitable for competitions. Rustic poles will last longer if the bark is removed.

Semi-gloss paint is the most suitable finish. No undercoat will be needed when it comes to repainting or touching up, and it also dries quickly and gives less reflection on sunny days.

Any slats used for making wings or fillers should be less than 4 in (10 cm) or more than 8 in (20 cm) apart so that a horse's leg cannot become trapped between them. For schooling at home and for practice fences the simplest standard (wing) to make is one with a $4\frac{1}{2} \times 2\frac{1}{4}$ in (11 cm $\times$ 5.5 cm) post on cross-feet. However, this will not be acceptable for a competition unless it has additional decoration to form wings at either side. There is also the problem of fitting fillers under the poles because the cross-feet are in the way.

The most commonly used designs for wings are illustrated on pages 229 and 230. The sloping side is more economical on timber. For the wing with both sides of the same length cup holes can be drilled on either support post, avoiding having to match the left and right-hand pairs. It can also incorporate a variety of designs. Cup holes can be drilled 4 in (10 cm) to 2 in (5 cm) apart. The latter is more suitable for competition use.

If the fences are to be transported regularly, or if they are to be stored where space is limited, the feet of the wings and the feet on

Detail of schooling standard

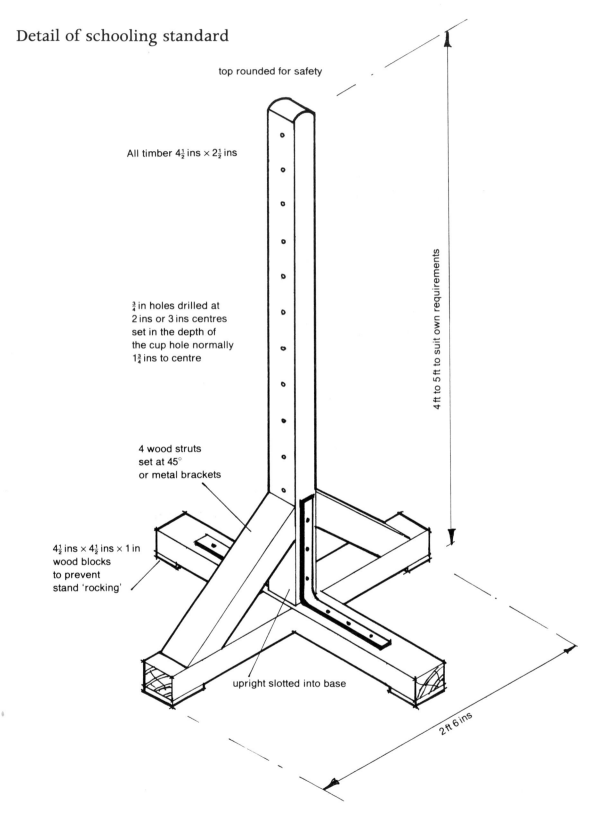

top rounded for safety

All timber 4½ ins × 2½ ins

¾ in holes drilled at
2 ins or 3 ins centres
set in the depth of
the cup hole normally
1¾ ins to centre

4 wood struts
set at 45°
or metal brackets

4½ ins × 4½ ins × 1 in
wood blocks
to prevent
stand 'rocking'

4 ft to 5 ft to suit own requirements

upright slotted into base

2 ft 6 ins

Detail of standard wing and foot

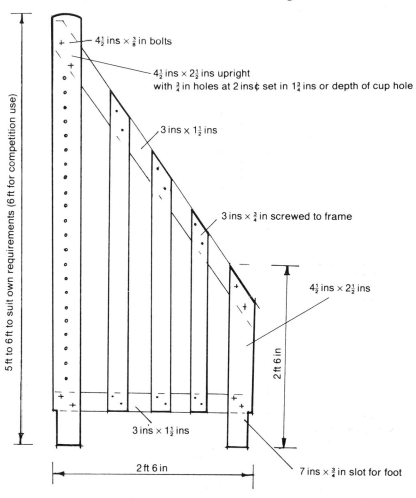

$4\frac{1}{2}$ ins × $\frac{3}{8}$ in bolts

$4\frac{1}{2}$ ins × $2\frac{1}{2}$ ins upright
with $\frac{3}{4}$ in holes at 2 ins¢ set in $1\frac{3}{4}$ ins or depth of cup hole

3 ins × $1\frac{1}{2}$ ins

3 ins × $\frac{3}{4}$ in screwed to frame

$4\frac{1}{2}$ ins × $2\frac{1}{2}$ ins

2 ft 6 in

5 ft to 6 ft to suit own requirements (6 ft for competition use)

3 ins × $1\frac{1}{2}$ ins

2 ft 6 in

7 ins × $\frac{3}{4}$ in slot for foot

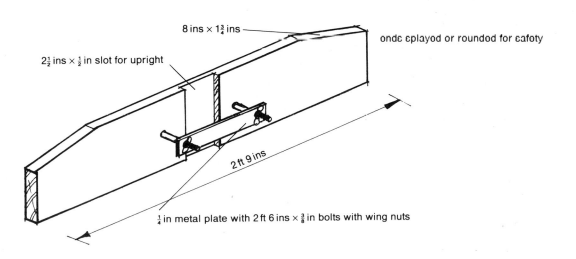

8 ins × $1\frac{3}{4}$ ins

ends splayed or rounded for safety

$2\frac{1}{2}$ ins × $\frac{1}{2}$ in slot for upright

2 ft 9 ins

$\frac{1}{4}$ in metal plate with 2 ft 6 ins × $\frac{3}{8}$ in bolts with wing nuts

any fillers should be removable. Otherwise they can be permanently bolted on.

The constructruction of brush boxes has already been shown on page 108. Other fillers can include wooden walls or hanging panels. They can be any height, according to requirements, but 2 ft (61 cm) ones are the easiest to cut out of standard plywood sheets. They should never be less than $\frac{1}{2}$ in (12 mm) thick, otherwise horses may put their feet through them.

Metal and plastic cups are available from most suppliers of show jumping equipment, or they can be home-made if the right materials are available. There are various designs, of which one of the simplest is shown on page 232 with a 6 in × $\frac{1}{2}$ in (15 cm × 12 mm) bolt used in place of a pin.

Detail of standard wing

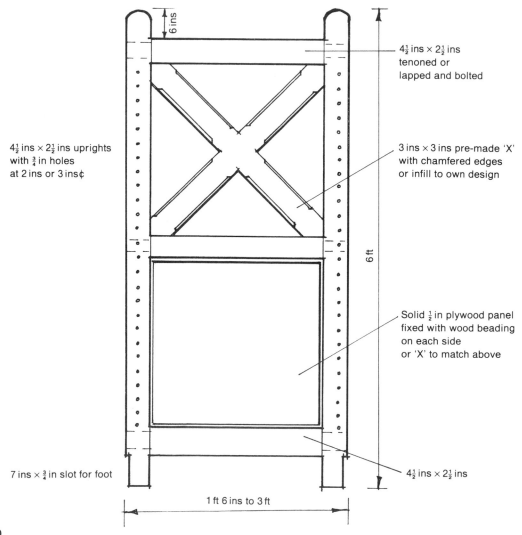

6 ins

$4\frac{1}{2}$ ins × $2\frac{1}{2}$ ins
tenoned or
lapped and bolted

$4\frac{1}{2}$ ins × $2\frac{1}{2}$ ins uprights
with $\frac{3}{4}$ in holes
at 2 ins or 3 ins¢

3 ins × 3 ins pre-made 'X'
with chamfered edges
or infill to own design

6 ft

Solid $\frac{1}{2}$ in plywood panel
fixed with wood beading
on each side
or 'X' to match above

7 ins × $\frac{3}{4}$ in slot for foot

$4\frac{1}{2}$ ins × $2\frac{1}{2}$ ins

1 ft 6 ins to 3 ft

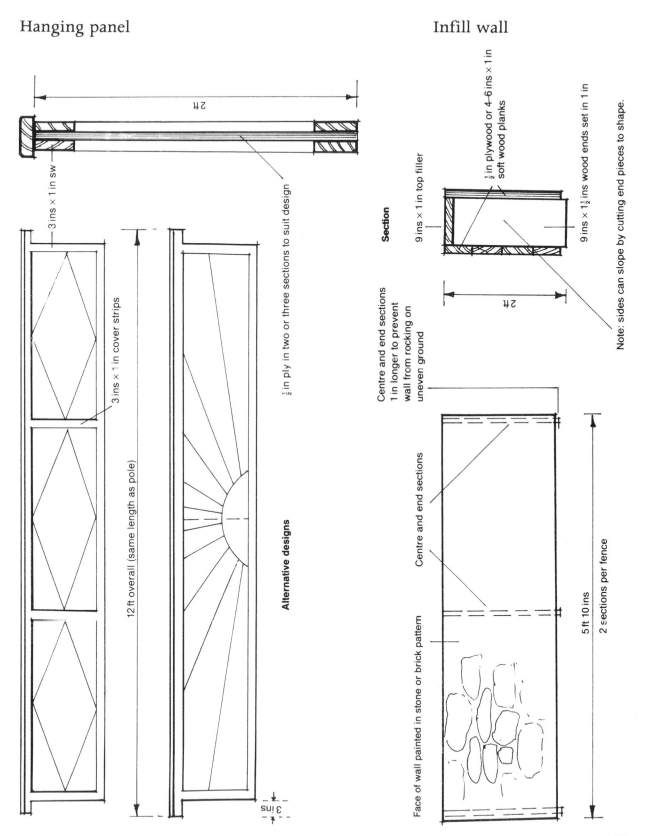

Hanging panel

3 ins × 1 in sw

2 ft

½ in ply in two or three sections to suit design

3 ins × 1 in cover strips

12 ft overall (same length as pole)

Alternative designs

3 ins

Infill wall

Section

½ in plywood or 4–6 ins × 1 in soft wood planks

9 ins × 1 in top filler

9 ins × 1½ ins wood ends set in 1 in

Note: sides can slope by cutting end pieces to shape.

2 ft

Centre and end sections 1 in longer to prevent wall from rocking on uneven ground

Centre and end sections

Face of wall painted in stone or brick pattern

5 ft 10 ins

2 sections per fence

Detail of pole cup

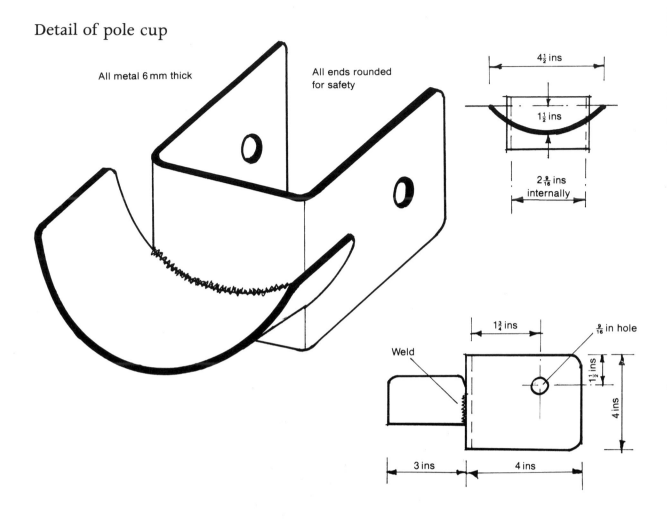

All metal 6 mm thick

All ends rounded for safety

$4\frac{1}{2}$ ins

$1\frac{1}{2}$ ins

$2\frac{9}{16}$ ins internally

$1\frac{3}{4}$ ins

$\frac{9}{16}$ in hole

Weld

$1\frac{1}{2}$ ins

4 ins

3 ins

4 ins

Acknowledgements

Neil Ayer would like to thank the following for the contributions they made to his chapter: Jack Burton, Gary Carmichael, Pete Costello, Roger Haller, Jack Le Goff, Patrick Lynch, Chris Milanesi, Richard Newton, Hugh Thomas, and James Wofford.

Illustration credits

Photographs:
Philip Herbert: pages 52, 53, 54, 55, 56, 57, 60, 61, 63, 64, 67, 68, 72, 73, 74, 78, 80, 83, 84, 85 (top), 90 (bottom), 91, 92, 93, 96, 97, 98, 99, 102 (bottom, 106, 107, 111, 112, 113, 115, 116, 117, 120, 121, 122, 123, 124, 125, 126, 127, 129, 130, 131, 132, 133, 134, 135, 136, 137, 138, 141, 142, 143, 144, 145, 172, 173, 174, 175. Kit Houghton: 8, 26, 27, 58, 59, 65, 82, 86, 90 (top), 95, 105, 119, 149, 186, 202. Cyril Diamond: 48, 100, 101. John Evetts: 192. Peter Harding: 51. Richard Jeffery: 216, 223, 224, 225. Neil Jones: 85 (bottom), 104. Marston Photographics: 102 (top).
Diagrams and drawings:
Alan Hamp: pages 32, 33, 35, 37, 38, 40, 41, 42, 44, 45, 81, 154, 155, 160, 161, 164, 165, 176, 180, 184, 198, 199, 201, 203, 212, 213, 214, 215, 218, 219, 220. Mark Gibbs: 69, 70, 71, 77, 79, 80, 86, 94, 99, 101, 107, 118. Julian Seaman: 31, 82, 87, 88, 89, 114, 149, 150. Richard Jeffery: 228, 229, 230, 231, 232. Sue Carlton: 156. Mary Young: 152, 162.

Index

A

Aerial photographs of the site, 23
Alluvial soil, and course design, 18
Alternatives, in cross-country
    courses, 151, 153–156
Angled fences, 42
Arch, railed, 101–103
Artificial brush fence, 114–118
Artificial ditches, 128
Artificial take-off and landing
    areas, 19
Axe, 62

B

Balustrade, 90
Barrels, 103
Birch fences, 108–118
Bolt cutters, 61
Bounce fences, 41
Bow saw, 58
Brace, carpenter's, 61
Brush fences, 46, 104–108
    artificial, 114–118
Brush fences (see also Birch
    fences), 46, 104–108, 114–118
Bullfinch fences, 114

C

Car parking, 23
Carpenter's brace, 61
Chain, towing, 62
Chainsaw, 52–53
Chalkland, and course design, 18

Checking the course, 171
Churn stand, 97
Claw hammer, 56
Clay land, and course design,
    17–18
Coffins, 39
    distances between, 169
Combinations,
    for cross-country, 151, 157–166,
    167
    for show jumping, 211–217
Communications,
    in cross-country competitions,
    171, 179–181
    in show jumping competitions,
    209
Competitions, cross-country,
    checking the course and fences,
    171
    class and siting of fences, 28
    communications, 171, 179–181
    control system, 179–181
    course repairs and adjustments,
    179
    flags and other markers,
    174–177
    penalty zones, 178
    roping, 177, 178
    spectators, 177–178
    start and finish area, 24,
    171–173, 185
Coniferous timber, 67
Corners, 42
Corsican pine timber, 67
Course design, (cross-country),
    17–29
    aerial photographs, 23

aesthetic appearance, 23
aim of the course, 15
area required, 22
bad courses, 43
choice of terrain, 17–20
clover-leaf pattern, 22
degree of difficulty, 15–16
distances between obstacles,
   168–170
general principles, 13–16, 43,
   166–167
the ideal course, 43
and land use, 19
maps of the site, 23–24
natural features, 20–21
object of the course, 30
and obstacle construction,
   30–43
points to remember, 166–167
and rules of competition, 24–25
safety, 14–15
siting the fences, 26–29, 36
summary, 43
turns, 22–23
use of terrain, 21–25
Course design, (show jumping),
   207–232
Cross-country, 11–194
   competition organisation and
     control, 171–181
   constructing the obstacles,
     47–150
   designing the course, 17–29
   designing the obstacles, 30–46
   options, alternatives and
     combinations, 151–167
   principles of course design,
     13–16
   recommended distances,
     168–170
   rider's view of the course,
     189–194
   three-day events, 182–188,
     193–194
Crowbar, 56

D

Designing cross-country courses,
   17–29
Designing cross-country obstacles,
   30–46

metal cans, 45
ornamental, 101
palisade, 46
portable, 46
schooling, 45
seat type, 46
siting of, 26–29, 36
spacing of, 28, 48, 164
spread, 40
steeplechase, 118–119, 186–188
Designing show jumping courses,
   207–232
Distances between obstacles,
   recommended, 168–170
Ditches and banks, 41, 120–135
   artificial ditches, 128
   digging ditches by machine, 128
   distances between obstacles, 169
   ditches 'away' and 'towards'
     obstacles, 84
   natural ditches, 120
   reducing ditch width, 127–128
   revetting a ditch, 123–125
   Trakehner, 84
Dressage, 195–204
   arena, 23, 197–204
   choosing a site, 197–198
   decoration of arena, 204
   judges, 203–204
   laying out an arena, 198–199
   materials for arena, 200–203
   setting up a large arena,
     199–200
   setting up a small arena,
     198–199
Drop fences, 39

E

Elephant trap, 86

F

Fences,
   angled, 42
   birch, 46, 108–118
   bounce, 41
   brush, 46, 104–108, 114–118
   bullfinch, 114
   checking, 171
   coffins, 39

corners, 42, 95
degree of difficulty, 28–29
ditches, 41
drop, 39
hayrack, 46
on hills and slopes, 36, 49–50
hurdles, 45
ideal first fence, 43
island, 96–103
materials, 26–28
stile, 90–91
straw bales, 45, 103
studying before competition, 190–193
table-type, 46, 99
turns, 42–43
walls, 103–104
water, 42
(scc also Obstacles)
Fencing mall, 62
Fencing pliers, 56
Flags,
on cross-country course, 174–177
on show jumping course, 223
for signalling in competitions, 179
turning, on steeplechase courses, 187

G

Gates, wooden, 100–101
Going, 17–20
consistency of, 20
effects of land types on, 17–20
ideal, 18
Grassland, and course design, 19–20
Ground (see Going)

H

Hammer, claw, 56
Hanging panel, 231
Hardwood timber, 67
Hayrack fence, 46, 92
Hedges (see Birch fences and Brush fences)
Helsinki steps, 82–83
Hills and slopes, 20–21, 22

and construction of obstacles, 49–50
and siting of obstacles, 36
Horse sense and course design, 13
Horses,
consideration for when designing obstacles, 30–31
and degrees of difficulty, 33–35
weight of, and effect on going, 20
Hunter trials, and siting fences, 28
Hurdles, 45, 103

I

Infill wall, 231
Island fences, 96–103

J

Jack, high-lift, 62
Jemmy, 56–58

L

Land types, and cross-country course design, 17–23
Land use, and cross-country course design, 19
Lever, turning, 62
Limestone soil, and course design, 18
Loam, and course design, 18

M

Machinery, for building obstacles, 52–54
Maps,
and planning cross-country courses, 23–24
and planning show-jumping courses, 210–211
and walking the course, 190
Measuring stick, 58–61

N

Nails, 64
Natural features, and course
    design, 20–21
Normandy Bank, 163
Norwegian spruce timber, 67
Novice Events,
    and alternatives, 153
    and show jumping
        combinations, 211–212

O

Obstacle design, (cross-country),
    30–46
    dangerous obstacles, 35–36
    easy and difficult obstacles,
        32–35
    and the horse, 30–31, 33–35
    object of the course, 30
    siting, 36
    variety, 31
Obstacle design, (show jumping),
    210–221
Obstacles, (cross-country),
    birch fences, 108–118
    brush fences, 104–118
    constructing, 47–150
        equipment for, 51–65
        general points, 47–50
        labour for, 50
        machinery for, 52–54
        materials for, 26–28, 47–49
        money matters, 47
        and safety, 47–49
        tools for, 56–65
        vehicles for, 51–52
    designing, 30–46
    ditches and banks, 120–135
    posts and rails, 70–103
    spacing of, 28, 164
    steeplechase fences, 118–119,
        186–188
    types, 70–150
    walls, 103–104
    water, 139–150
    wings, 69
Obstacles (show jumping),
    constructing, 222–232
    designing, 210–221
Obstacles, (see also Fences)

Oil, 61
One-day event,
    and fence siting, 28
    placing of dressage arena, 23
    and walking the course,
        190–191
Options, 151–153
Options, alternatives and
    combinations, 151–167
Ornamental fences, 101
Oxers, for show jumping, 217, 219

P

Palisade fence, 46, 90
Penalty zones, at competitions, 178
Pheasant feeder, 100
Pliers, fencing, 56
Plumber's stilsons, 61
Pole cup, detail of, 232
Portable fences or frames, 46, 114
Post-driver, 54
    and safety, 75
Post-hole borer, 53–54
Posts and rails, 70–103
    for alternative and combination
        fences, 94–96
    distances between obstacles,
        168–170
    methods of construction, 75–81
    raising and lowering, 81
Preliminary Events, and
    alternatives, 153
Principles of course design, 13–16
Props, forked, 64

R

Rabbit holes, 19–20
Radios, 181
Rails, lightweight, 79–81
Railway sleepers (ties), 68, 96, 97
Rake, 62
Rasp, 61
Repairs during competitions, 179
Revetting,
    banks, 128–135
    ditches, 123–125
    drops, steps and banks, 128
Rivers, and course design, 20
Roof or railed arch, 101–103

Roping,
    at cross-country competitions,
        177, 178
    on steeplechase course, 187

S

Sacks, 103
Safety,
    and course design, 14–15
    and show jumping fences, 221
Sand-based soil, and course
        design, 18
Saw, bow, 58
Sawn rails, 81
Schooling fences, 45
Schooling standard, detail of, 228
Scots pine timber, 67
Seat fence, 46, 92
Shark's teeth, 91
Shears, 61
Shovel, 62
Show jumping, 205–232
    arena, 207–208
    building the course, 221–226
    combinations, 211–213
    completed course plan, 215
    course designer's brief, 207
    distances in combinations,
        212–213
    draft course plan, 214
    equipment and materials,
        208–209
    fence types, 218, 219
    making your own show jumps,
        227
    officials, 209
    planning and designing the
        course, 209–221
    ring, and planning the site, 23
    safety notes, 221
    types of jump, 217–221
Slasher, 62
Sledgehammer, 58
Sleeper fences,
    sleeper table and churn stand, 97
    sloping, 96
    sleeper wall, 96
Spade, 56
Spanners, 61, 64
Spectators, at competitions,
    177–178

Spread fences, 40
Staples, 65
Start and finish area, 24, 171–173,
    185
Steeplechase, 186–188
    and course design, 25
    fences for, 118–119
    roping the course, 187
Steps and banks, distances
        between obstacles, 169
Stile fence, 90–91
Stone-based soil, and course
        design, 18
Stopping points, 181
Straw bales, 45, 103
    for artificial brush fences,
        114–117
Streams, and course design,
    20
Surform, 61

T

Table fences, 46, 99
Take-off and landing areas, 22,
    33–34
    artificial, 19
Tape-measure, 58
Telegraph poles, 66
Television cameras, 21, 28
Terram, 19
Three-day events, 182–188
    cross-country box, 183–185
    roads and tracks, 182–183
    steeplechase, 186–188
    trading areas, 23
    walking the course, 193–194
Tiger trap, 86
Timber, 28, 49, 65–70
    dimensions, 68–70
    types of, 67–68
Timber wagon obstacle, 103
Tommy bar, 61
Tongs, timber-lifting, 62
Tools, and obstacle construction,
    56–65
Tow chain, 62
Trakehner obstacles, 84
Triple bars, for show jumping,
    220, 221
Trough, 99
Turning lever, 62

Turns, 42–43
    and course design, 22–23
Tyres, 103

V

Vehicles, and obstacle
    construction, 51–52
Verticals, for show jumping,
    217–218
Volcanic soil, and course design, 18

W

Walking the course, 189–194

Walls, 103–104
    infill, 231
Waste product timber, 67–68
Water obstacles, 42, 139–150
    placement in combinations, 163
Weather,
    and course design, 14
    and the going, 18–19
Weighing tent, 173
Wings, 69, 229, 230
Wire, 64
Wire brush, 61
Wire cutters, 61
Wooden gates, 100–101
Woodland, and course design, 20